Welcome Home, Charlie!

STEPHAN D. FALES

COPYRIGHT © 2025
Stephan D. Fales

All rights are reserved. No part of this book may be reproduced, distributed, or transmitted in any form or by any means, including photocopying, recording, or other electronic or mechanical methods, without the prior written permission of the author, except in the case of brief quotations embodied in critical reviews and certain other noncommercial uses permitted by copyright law. For permission requests, write to the author at the address provided in the acknowledgments section of this book.

Printed in the United States of America

Acknowledgment

I want to thank the people who made this journey possible. To my mom and dad, Sharon and Harold Fales—thank you for fostering my love of reading from the very beginning. To my wife, Elizabeth Fales, whose unwavering support carried me through every chapter, revision, and doubt. To Jen Braaksma, my brilliant book coach and editor, for helping me shape this story with clarity and heart. And most of all, to my 5th grade class at Stuttgart Elementary School in Stuttgart, Germany (2024-2025)—your energy, curiosity, and joy reignited my passion for storytelling. This book exists because of you.

Contents

Acknowledgment V

Chapter One: Born In The Shadows 2

Chapter Two: The Empty Hideout 6

Chapter Three: Flooded Memories 11

Chapter Four: Predators In The Dark 14

Chapter Five: Wounds And Warnings 19

Chapter Six: Blue Eyes, Kind Hands 23

Chapter Seven: A Name Of My Own 29

Chapter Eight: The Call Of The Barn 35

Chapter Nine: Charlene's Tears 41

Chapter Ten: Among The Cattle And The Goat 47

Chapter Eleven: Welcome To The Barn Family 53

Chapter Twelve : Doors Opening, Bonds Forming 58

Chapter Thirteen: Adventures With Peanut 67

Chapter Fourteen: The Distance Between Us 71

Chapter Fifteen: New Friends, Old Tensions 76

Chapter Sixteen: The Meaning Of Family 80

Chapter Seventeen: Charlene's Silence 83

Chapter Eighteen: Night In The Barn 88

Chapter Nineteen: Lessons From The Herd 93

Chapter Twenty: Guardian Of The Barnyard 100

Chapter Twenty-One: Between Freedom And Love 106

Chapter Twenty-Two: Whispers In The Straw 110

Chapter Twenty-Three: The Return Of Danger 114

Chapter Twenty-Four: Trust Tested 118

Chapter Twenty-Five: A Home In Two Worlds 123

Chapter Twenty-Six: Bridging The Divide 127

Chapter Twenty-Seven: Charlene's Forgiveness 132

Chapter Twenty-Eight: Finding Home 137

Chapter One:
Born in the Shadows

I was born in a field with my littermates. The aroma of grass, dirt, and mom's scent was my whole life for weeks. The scent of mother's milk clung to all of us, mixed with the pungent perfume of Mom's coat—a blend of dust, plant-sweetness, and something sour that made me hesitate each time I inhaled.

We were a mismatched group. None of us looked alike. My siblings' fur carried wild swirls of color, while mine was stark, divided—black and white in clean, bold patches. My belly was mostly white, with only the tips of my paws matching. My legs stood straight and black, like shadows, while my sides were splashed with chaotic patterns of both. I thought it was pretty cool, but I was different from the rest.

I remember wrestling with my siblings during Mom's long hours away from our hideout, tumbling in the tangled grass. Even though we played and wrestled, something never felt quite right. We were together, yet separate—just a collection of small bodies rolling through the grass, drawn together by instinct rather than true connection. I felt it when we settled for the night, curled in a huddle for warmth. I slept among them, but I never felt tethered. Maybe it was because I was different. My coat let me slip into the shadows, making me part of the landscape rather than part of them.

I used to watch the others and question whether I truly belonged. Something about me felt different, as though a secret had been stitched into my very fur. At night, when the world softened and dimmed, I would disappear into the darkness—swallowed by the shadows while they remained outlined in the fading light. It was as if the dusk itself recognized me, wrapping me in its embrace. I didn't know why, but I could feel it carried meaning. Perhaps I was meant to wander where they could not follow.

As we grew older we scattered into the field, each of us exploring different patches of earth and sky. Today, I had my eye on a creature clinging to a blade of grass, its tiny body twitching in the breeze. I watched it, muscles coiled, thinking only of the taste and the rush of the hunt.

Then the shadow came.

The hair on my neck raised, a prickling sensation running down my spine to the tip of my tail. I remained perfectly still, ears flicking to the distant, shrill cries from the trees. My prey was within reach. Instinct told me to strike, so I did. The insect crunched in my teeth, juices bursting into my mouth as I quickly swallowed. The thrill of catching something—of being a hunter—was satisfying.

And then, just as easily, I saw what it meant to be hunted.

A rush of air, a scream, then silence. I turned my head in time to see the winged creature lifting off, talons curled around my sibling's limp body. My muscles locked, every part of me braced—but I stayed where I was. The moment had already passed. There was no point in moving. It had already happened.

I dropped low to the ground, slipping deeper into the shadows, and quietly traced my steps back to the hideout. The number of us had changed. The loss felt distant, like watching a branch snap in the wind. One moment there, then gone.

Seeing the creature taking my sibling away, I felt drawn back toward our hideout. I'm wondering if the others are okay. I also feel a weird need to protect the others. I can smell dry dust, dirt, the fresh aroma of plants, and the strong, pungent scent of our hideout as I near.

The breeze stirs the leaves in the trees, but everything else is eerily still. I stop.

"Why is it so quiet?"

I decide to stay where I am, waiting for my siblings to appear. Lowering myself onto my paws, I rest—alert, ready to move if needed. The shadows stretch around me, wrapping me in their cover. Hidden, my breathing is slow and steady, my heart calm. The sun's warmth fades from my fur as the sky dims. "Still, nobody has returned."

I flick my ears, listening. Nothing. No rustling in the grass, no familiar scents drifting toward me. "Are they all waiting for a sign of survivors?"

I press my nose to the ground, inhaling deeply. "No fresh scent trails. No movement."

A strange heaviness settles in my chest.

Confident that I am unseen, I creep forward toward the hideout. Every four steps, I pause, flicking my ears to catch any sound. The sky darkens, swallowing the last traces of light. I scurry into the hideout, quickly turning to face the outside.

Silence.

I wait. I listen. I watch.

Nobody comes back.

The place feels empty. Cold.

I sniff the air again, searching for something—anything—that tells me I am not alone. But the only scent here is my own.

"What now?"

I crouch, tensed for a quick escape, my muscles coiled. The need to protect is gone, replaced by something heavier.

"I didn't mind being alone—until now. Now it feels like there's no choice. I am truly alone."

I close my eyes, pressing my body into the shadows. "Do I stay? Do I leave?"

For the first time, I realize—there is nothing keeping me here..

Chapter Two: The Empty Hideout

Images of warm bodies cuddled together—mother slipping in to feed us and then disappearing—danced through my restless dreams. The screech of a night hunter shattered the illusion, pulling me into wakefulness. I gazed into the darkness, watching for the predator.

Nobody has come back. At first light, I have to decide what to do.

I doze off again, but my mind won't stop.

I've always felt different. We weren't really a family—just a bunch of us trying to survive, side by side.

So why did I come back? What made me think I needed to protect anyone?

I'm alone now. It's up to me. I need food. I need shelter. I need to hunt.

A chilly wind hits my face and pulls me awake. Rain taps the ground around me. Morning's here, and the season is shifting—just enough to feel it.

Okay... first, food. Shelter can wait or change. I'll make my world out there, step by step.

I rise and shake off sleep, stretching from head to tail. "I really don't want to get wet!"

But staying dry isn't an option when hunger gnaws at me. "I must become the hunter."

I step into standing water, instantly soaked. The hunt feels pointless—but my stomach growls, and instinct pushes me forward.

I lope toward the open field, the tall cover fading into brittle stubble. No shelter. No hiding from the sky.

I break into a sprint, faster than ever. The tall grass ahead is my only hope. I dive in, spinning to scan the field behind me.

My heart pounds, breath hitching. I've never been this far. "Need to calm down and think."

I lower my belly to the wet ground, forcing myself to slow down, to listen. My surroundings feel still. Nothing moves across the field toward me.

"I'm sure I'm safe from that direction."

The sky shifts—a darkness creeping in like night, wind thrashing through the trees. Rain drives sideways in gusts, then stops and starts again, unpredictable and relentless.

I need to get out of this rain. I need warmth."

Moving away from the open field through the taller grass—I spot a building with lights.

There is no place to hide between the grass and the building. "If I want cover, I'll have to make a straight, fast dash to the edge."

I freeze! Something just came out of the building. It moves to another part of the structure and lifts a huge door.

Soon, there's a roaring sound and light spills out. A noise-maker with lights rolls from the opening, following a worn path before turning onto another hard surface and moving away.

"The door is still open."

I burst forward, running full speed for the opening. "Inside. No rain. Dry."

I shake violently, scattering droplets from my fur—relief giving way to shock.

Then the smells hit me. "Overwhelming. Suffocating."

My head spins. So many different scents, layered, clashing. "None of them are food."

"I can't stay here. This can't be safe."

Then—scratching. "Tiny feet moving close by."

Instinct takes over. My body shifts, crouching low. "A hunter again."

I glide toward the sound, ears flicking, listening. A strange scent drifts toward me—dry grass, something familiar yet misplaced.

"This is not the smell that almost made me faint. I know this scent. Why is it coming from that thing over there?"

I drop lower, only the tip of my tail twitching with the rhythm of my heartbeat. Every muscle tenses.

I stare at the object, convinced the noise of tiny feet came from beneath it.

Quietly, I sample the air. "There it is—the dust and sweet scent of prey. I just need to wait."

Then, its head slowly appears from the open space under the object.

I watch its tiny nose twitch, testing the air for danger. "Luckily, I'm upwind. My scent won't reach it."

I tense. "Just a little bit further."

Time crawls as it edges forward. Then—the perfect moment.

I launch, snapping my jaws around its neck just as it turns to flee. Victory!

Suddenly, light flares to life, blinding me.

I spin and bolt toward the opening. Back into the rain.

I dash around the building, searching for cover. A huge object looms ahead, draped in something slick and dripping.

I dive underneath, racing into the dry darkness, pressing deeper inside until I feel safe.

I drop to the ground, my prey still clutched in my mouth, silent.

My ears dance, scanning for trouble. Nothing but dampness in the air.

A muffled banging sounds in the distance, but no movement comes my way.

Calmness settles over me.

I am the hunter. It's time to eat.

Chapter Three: Flooded Memories

As I near the tall grass by the tree on the edge of the field, I hear water flowing.

I glide through the thick growth and step into a standing puddle.

Surprised, I step back, shaking one front paw, then the other. I stare ahead.

My hideout is filled with water.

I sit, stunned. Confused.

"No warmth. No siblings. No shelter."

I glance back across the open field toward the place I fled from. "I'm not going back that way."

I circle the edge of the flooded hideout.

Beyond it lies another open field, with more buildings in the distance.
A small sun hangs in the sky between them, casting a soft glow.

"I don't know why, but I feel drawn to that light."

Guided by its glow, I move forward.

The open field stretches wide, scattered with cut plant stubble—exposed again to hunters.

Finally, I reach tall growth once more.

I slip into the shadows—hidden. Safe.

I settle, scanning the scene in front of me.

A wide dirt path runs both left and right.

Ahead, a small path leads toward the buildings—toward the light perched atop a tall, leafless tree.

To the right, a long building glows, light spilling from inside. "I get the feeling of warmth."

To the left, a huge building looms in darkness.

"I wonder what's inside."

I decide to move closer.

Chapter Four: Predators in the Dark

I survey the path I need to cross.

"No protection. I have to move fast."

The tree looks like the best spot to run to.

Crickets chirp in the thick night air, their rhythmic songs weaving into the darkness. Flying insects pulse dim glows—flashes of light flickering above the grass.

Detecting no movement, I step cautiously from the tall growth at the side of the hard path.

The moment my paw touches the ground, I release all tension—exploding into a sprint toward the tree.

A small pole stands nearby, a box perched on top. I barely register it, locked onto my goal.

I leap into the grass between the tree and the pole, disappearing into the shadows. Hugging the ground, I wait. Listen. Anticipate.

Danger could strike at any moment.

My legs wobble beneath me, trembling from the sprint. My fur is damp—not from rain, but sweat.

I turn slowly, scanning the shadows, heart hammering in my chest.

The smells here are nothing like my hideout.

Earth. Grass. A sharp, unfamiliar scent of animals I've never met, wafting from the large building across the field.

The building with bright lights stands like a beacon in the evening darkness.

The harsh glow of the pole light casts long, twisting shadows across the grass—like reaching fingers.

"Okay. What do I do now?"

"I could move toward the nearest building. The strong smell of an unknown animal lingers there."

"But—other scents drift in from the second building. Scents that make my stomach twist and my mouth water."

"Food. It has to be food."

A slight breeze carries scents I don't recognize—heavy, wild, unfamiliar. I swallow hard. Nothing smells like the hideout or the field. "This is crazy. None of this feels right."

My ears twitch, swiveling toward unseen sounds. Only the wind brushing through the tall grass, whispering against my fur. The absence of night sounds is suffocating.

But something else lingers in the air—something animal. It's layered: salt, dirt, straw—deep and rich, it fills my nose. Then comes another scent—warm, mouthwatering, familiar. Food! My stomach clenches. It has been hours since I've eaten. The glow from a single building lights the darkness like a beacon.

"That structure over there—it smells of animals. I can't tell what kind. The other one glows like warmth... and food."

I flex my claws into the earth, thinking.

"The shadows might be the safest path to get a closer look."

But was I sure? Was anything safe anymore?

Stay low. Move slowly.

I scan the darkness, searching for any movement. Then, careful and controlled, I stand on all four paws.

I creep forward, hugging the edge of the looming structure's shadow. Every few steps, I drop into the grass, form tight to the earth. My eyes sweep from the shadows to the glowing building, watching for any flicker of movement.

The closer I get, the stronger the animal musk grows—salty, straw-scented. It wraps around me like an invisible presence, stirring unease and curiosity.

I mark it—an investigation for later. For now: food. Survival first.

A wire hangs low across the path. I dip my head beneath it and resume my slow, deliberate steps, crossing the grass under the shelter of darkness. My tail ticks like a clock as I scan the glowing house for any signs of life.

Then—from beyond the larger structure, at the edge of night—a sound. Sharp. Waiting.

My ears flick toward it. Muscles coil. I freeze. Heart hammering. Eyes lock on the deep dark beyond the building. Something is there.

I rise slowly to my paws; eyes fixed on the lights from the house. Then I tense, fur bristling. Something shifts in the air. A change. A warning.

Before I can react, something slams into my side. Hard. A force like thunder sends me rolling toward the large building. Alarms blare in my head. Instinct explodes.

WELCOME HOME, CHARLIE!

I spring up, teeth bared, swinging my head, searching—ready to strike. Out of the darkness comes a blur.

A flash of light off its teeth. A glint of yellow eyes.

It hits again—biting, clawing, relentless. The attack comes so fast all I can do is cover up and try to survive.

"Rowl!" I scream, my voice breaking through the night.

Pain explodes through my body. But worse—worse than the pain—is the weight. The crushing power.

I've fought before. I've bled before. But this is different.

I sink my teeth into the creature's nearest paw.

It yanks away. I barely register it—my vision spinning—until I am forced to meet its eyes.

Burning yellow. Teeth. Closer. Coming.

"Rowl!" I scream again as it tears into my shoulder, claws ripping down my side like fire.

I twist, scramble, desperate to crawl away.

Then—a sharp crack. The air snaps with electricity.

A burst of light. Heat. A scream—high, sharp. Not mine.

The smell hits first—bitter, acrid. Burnt fur.

My attacker tears away into the darkness.

I don't move. I just lay there, panting. Dazed. Heart hammering against the inside of my ribs.

Alive. Somehow, still alive..

Chapter Five: Wounds and Warnings

I lay sprawled in the grass, breath ragged, limbs trembling. Pain pulses through every inch of me in sharp, unforgiving waves. My paws brush the earth—cool soil and broken blades, damp and rough against raw skin.

Fear. Rage. Shame.

I'd been caught off guard. That attack was faster than anything I'd ever faced.

And I didn't understand it.

Its scent was like nothing I'd ever known. The vicious bites, the ripping claws. And those yellow eyes—etched into memory like scars.

My unfocused gaze falls upon the wire, blurred in the dim light. It hovers—wrong, unnatural—strung as if by invisible hands with cruel intent.

Suspended and taut. Motionless.

Like a predator waiting for its next strike.

A rancid smell claws at my nostrils—bitter, choking. It pours from the wire like rot, making my stomach twist.

The wire had been there. Watching. Witnessing.

Had it struck my assailant?

Had it sparked, burned, defended me?

The thought chills me—and, strangely, calms me.

If it had hurt the creature... it had protected me.

Its menace had turned guardian.

I am still bleeding. Still broken.

But my eyes stay fixed on the wire. Hypnotized.

Wary. Its silent power looms, a reminder that even in the worst moments, salvation can come from the most unlikely threats.

Through the fog of pain, a ping-ping sound reaches my ears. I have to find its source. Maybe shelter. Somewhere to rest.

Each step is a struggle against gravity. My limbs drag—heavy, sluggish—as if the ground itself wants to keep me.

Slowly, I move toward the sound.

I cross a hard path, passing the large building's door. My body feels hollow, barely holding together beneath me.

I am close—I know it. But there is no way in.

The pinging echoes nearby... yet stays out of reach.

Exhaustion claws at me.

I collapse. Still, I force myself to crawl—just one more corner.

Then the ground changes beneath me: grass to dirt.

The smell thickens—wild, sharp, alive.

Too many scents press into my nose like invisible claws.

I lift my head and spot a dark opening in the building's side. Inside: rustling noises. Animals shifting, breathing heavy.

I'm not afraid.

I'm drawn.

The pinging comes from within. This is it.

I keep crawling—safety close enough to taste.

The hard earth gives way beneath me to soft, dry bedding.

In deep shadow, my body meets the wall. Slow. Unfeeling.

The ping-ping rings out nearby. But my strength is gone. The bedding welcomes me—warm, rich, steady.

I sink into it. Limbs aching. Thoughts distant. Surrendering before I can think.

Rustling surrounds me. Real. Alive.

I let go.

Melt into the soft ground.

A breath—long, deep, unsteady.

I am still aching. Still afraid.

But I am alive.

For now, that is enough.

Chapter Six:
Blue Eyes, Kind Hands

A voice pulls me from the haze of exhaustion.

A high-pitched squeal jolts me awake.

My fur bristles. My heart hammers against my ribs.

I snap my eyes open—locked into her eyes.

Blue.

A color I had seen only in open skies and endless horizons.

Yet somehow, those eyes hold me still.

I'm not afraid.

She isn't my sibling, but there is something familiar in her gaze. A quietness. A knowing.

Her joy presses through the air like warmth, wrapping around me in ways I don't understand.

"Daddy, look! A cat!"

A voice, full of excitement and wonder, yet edged with concern.

"What?"
A deeper voice responds—rougher, uncertain.

"Look, right there! A cat!"

I had been running, hiding, fighting to survive. But now, looking into her bright blue eyes—soft, kind, full of hope—something shifts inside me.

The fear loosens its grip.

The joy in her gentle expression melts it away.

I watch as her face shifts from surprise to worry, a pained look as she realizes I'm hurt.

"Don't touch it!" scolds the husky voice.

She bends down on one knee for a closer look, stretching her hands out to pick me up.

"But Dad, it's hurt," she whispers.

A shadow falls over us.

Massive. Still. Blocking the light.

I turn my head slowly, my heart ticking faster again.

The man is huge—broad-shouldered, wearing a cap pulled down low. He doesn't speak. Just stares at me.

Slowly, he kneels beside his daughter, pushing his cap back.

His face is stone. Hard lines. A wall.

But his eyes—His eyes are alive. Steely blue. Piercing. Curious.

He is looking at me. Really looking.

And suddenly, I don't feel quite so small.

I remember the feeling—like the farmer could see my heart beating in my chest.

I'm sure those eyes miss nothing, even though they never seem to move.

But I'm not afraid anymore.

Something about the humans—the way she looks at me, the way he doesn't flinch—makes me feel safe. Wanted. Protected.

The farmer speaks in a slow, even tone.

"Charlene, he's in rough shape."

"Oh, Daddy, can't we do anything?" she pleads.

"I don't know, sweetie," he says, giving his head a small shake.

"Please try, Daddy," she begs again, softer this time.

He sighs. "Honey, this little thing probably crawled in here to die in peace."

He studies me. "Looks like he tangled with a fox—those bite marks are deep. Nasty tears along the shoulder, too." His eyes stay steady, practiced. "He's got some bad wounds."

They share something wordless—a look, a hug, a quiet understanding that passes between them like breath.

My muscles begin to relax. My breathing steadies.

The war inside my body dulls to a murmur.

I've never felt this before in our hideout. There, we survived. Here—I am something more.

"Okay, Honey, we'll try," says the farmer.

"You run to the house and have Mom call the veterinarian. I'll bring this little one in right behind you." He gives her a small pat to send her on her way.

The farmer gently lifts me from Charlene's arms, careful not to aggravate my wounds. He carries me to a small table near the door, left wide open after Charlene ran out.

He sets me on the table. I roll onto my uninjured side, laying my head down.

Tired. Anxious. Watching his practiced motion.

"I'm just going to look at your scratches," he says gently. "I won't hurt you."

I feel his hands on my side. I wince and lift my head to look. He cleans the blood from my fur.

"Well, I think you gave that fox a struggle. These are long but not very deep."

He applies something cool to the wound.

I flinch, but don't pull away. His touch isn't like claws. It calms more than it hurts.

Just as he finishes patching me up, another person arrives.

"Mr. Branch, I hear you found an injured cat this morning," a soft voice says kindly.

"Hi Dr. Wood, I didn't find this cat. Charlene found it in our cattle stalls, in the straw," explains Mr. Branch.

I turn to look. A woman older than Charlene but younger than Mr. Branch gazes at me with kind eyes and a calm demeanor.

She approaches and examines the work Mr. Branch has done. "You did nice work with those scratches, Mr. Branch," she acknowledges.

"Let's see what we have here," she says softly, checking the bite wounds.
Her hands move with quiet precision, steady and sure, the scent of antiseptic mixing with the hay-dusted air.

"I'll need to put him to sleep and do some work to make sure the muscles and ligaments aren't damaged. Clean it out a little to stop infection," she explains.

Charlene returns with a blanket.

"What? You can't do it here?" she asks, her voice tight with concern.

"Charlene, it's not our cat. Dr. Wood has all the material to take care of this easily in her office," assures Mr. Branch.

"Dad! She has all of her medical stuff in her truck. Why can't we just get it done here? Then I can take care of our new cat," insists Charlene.

I watch as Mr. Branch and the doctor look at each other. His stance softens. The doctor smiles.

"Okay, Charlene. I'll get my stuff from the truck," Dr. Wood assures her.

"You can use this table. I'll get some towels," Mr. Branch agrees.

"That's alright. I have pads in the truck I can place on the table," Dr. Wood replies, stepping out.

Charlene stands beside me, her fingers brushing gently over my fur.

"You're going to be okay," she whispers, as if willing the words to make it true.

And for the first time, I almost believe it.

Chapter Seven: A Name of My Own

I woke up, groggy, unsure where I was. I was lying on my side, the surface beneath me hard and cold.

My left shoulder felt heavy, like something was pressing down on it, but I didn't want to pick up my head to check.

Then I heard it-the same ping-ping sound I had followed into the building.

The air carried the familiar scent of dust, sweat, and straw. I was still inside.

There was another familiar sound, but I could not make it out. It seemed like a soft, gentle whisper.

I tried to focus my eyes toward the whisper. It was Charlene, whispering to me. I could tell by her face she was a little worried.

Then I heard her whisper again. "Charlie, Charlie, it's okay, I'm right here."

I felt her hand gently brush my head and travel down the full length of my back. She did this with a slow rhythm multiple times. It felt so good, I gave her a low "purr" of thanks.

I heard her call," Hey, Dad! Charlie is waking up."

I heard steps come into the room. The smell of manure, animal scent, grass, and dust followed through the door.

"Who is Charlie?" came the husky voice I now recognized as Mr. Branch's.

"Well, I named our new cat Charlie because it is a boy cat and I wanted to name it after me," explained Charlene.

I could see Mr. Branch's blue eyes twinkle. Then he said, "Our new cat?"

"Well, Dr. Wood said it would need a few weeks to heal. There was no collar on it, and I found it in our barn," reasoned Charlene, still gently stroking my fur.

I watched them both look at each other, then look at me. I saw Mr. Branch nod," Ok. Charlie is your new cat. You have to take care of him. That includes cleaning the cat box. I don't want my house smelling like a cat box."

Charlene grabbed her dad with a big hug. "I will do everything for Charlie, I promise."

As Charlene hugged her dad, I let out a soft breath I didn't know I'd been holding.

I had a name. I had a place. For the first time, I wasn't just surviving.

Over the next few weeks, Charlene became my shadow.

She was there when I opened my eyes, there when I drifted off again. She fed me from a tiny glass dropper, drop by drop, her hand steady, voice soft. I didn't know food could taste like kindness until then. Eventually, I found the strength to chew real food—and Charlene beamed like I'd won a prize.

WELCOME HOME, CHARLIE!

Under her watchful eyes and gentle touch, I healed. Slowly. Steadily. Some days I ached. Some days I slept too much. But each morning I felt stronger—and somehow, safer.

And then... we played.

I never thought I'd enjoy playing again. But Charlene made everything feel like a game—her laughter pulled me in like a string. I pounced, darted, rolled, and swatted at her hands. She'd giggle when I stood up on my hind legs like a bear, then squeal when I sprang backward in mock retreat. She dangled a piece of yarn just out of reach, her eyes dancing with mischief. I chirped my protest. She grinned and flicked it away again.

Sometimes I let her win. Sometimes I didn't.

And when I played alone, I still felt her presence nearby. I'd stalk stuffed mice behind the couch or fish old bits of ribbon from under the chair. I liked having things to hunt—even if they didn't fight back.

When I wasn't chasing shadows, I was sleeping. My favorite place? Curled up in the crook of Charlene's arm, her breath slow and warm against my fur. But when she wasn't around, a patch of sun would do just fine.

Charlene made life... easy. Almost suspiciously easy. My bowl was never empty. Water is always fresh. Snacks appeared like magic.

And every now and then, when she scratched behind my ears just right, I thought:

Not bad for a cat who almost lost everything.

Charlene would bring her friends over after school—Indiana and Scout. They'd spread out their notebooks, chatter about teachers, play music too loud, and laugh like they'd invented fun.

The first time they visited, she picked me up and announced, "Hey everyone, meet my new cat—Charlie!"

She held me snug, proud as anything.

"I named him after me—but since he's a boy, I changed it to Charlie instead of Charlene."

"Hi, Charlie," the girls chimed in unison, reaching to pet me with curious fingers.

"Did you get him from a pet store?" Indiana asked.

"I like his markings," Scout added, trailing her fingers through the white-and-black patches on my side. "It's like spilled paint."

I felt Charlene's body shift slightly beneath me. Something in her shoulders tensed.

"I didn't buy him," she said, voice soft, unsure.

"I found him."

"Found him?" Indiana tilted her head. "Where?"

"In the barn one morning," Charlene replied, brushing my fur absently. "He was curled up in the straw. Barely moving."

"At first I thought he was just asleep," she went on, her voice dropping. "But then I saw the wounds. I got down close and realized how bad they were."

I felt her hand pause on my side—right over the scars.

"My dad patched up the scratches, and we called the vet. She fixed his shoulder—there were bite marks."

Scout ran a finger through my fur again. "No collar?"

"Nope," Charlene answered a little fast.

Indiana raised an eyebrow. "Did you put out a lost cat ad?"

Charlene hesitated for half a breath. "No... but we've had him for more than four weeks. Nobody's come looking." Scout looked at Indiana. Then back at me.

"Well," she said, "he's yours now."

Indiana smiled and nodded. "And honestly? I don't think he'd want to be anywhere else."

Charlene beamed. I tucked my head under her chin.

I didn't understand every word they said, but I felt it—Charlene was proud of me. And a little protective, too.

Maybe being someone's cat meant more than soft beds and full bowls.

Maybe it meant being worth standing up for.

Chapter Eight: The Call of the Barn

I loved being in Charlene's arms. They reminded me of the warmth I felt cuddled together with my siblings, like the warmth of the straw.

When Charlene wasn't home, I would stare out the window that faced the barn for hours.

Watching the barn stand firm against the breeze. It was more than just a place—it was a memory, a feeling, a call I couldn't ignore.

My memory of that night in the barn, the warmth of the straw, the feeling of being tugged at my heart. I felt that I belonged in the barn.

I could remember the scents of dirt, animals, straw, hay, grass, all things I understood.

Charlene's mother, Mrs. Branch, unknowingly helped foster my desire for the barn. Every day she would open the windows to freshen the house.

I could hear the window slide open. I would quickly move to the breeze as the aroma of earth, hay, and something wild drifted in, filling my lungs, stirring something deep inside me.

I would squeeze into the windowsill, my body pressed against the screen. Every rustling leaf, every distant whinny, every whiff of hay carried me back—back to where I felt I belonged. The barn called to me—softly at first, then louder with every passing breeze. My paws twitched, ears flicked, heart stirred. How long before I had to answer?

I could tell the weather had changed. There were more days that Mrs. Branch would open the windows. The breezes were bringing a warmth with all the scents. There were familiar smells of the old field.

One day, Mrs. Branch surprised me.

"Hi Charlie, let's give you some time outside," she stated.

I was surprised again when she connected something around my neck. Then picked me up and carried me outside the door.

Looking right at the barn!

"You will like this. A little sun and I'm sure you can find the shade to stay cool," she advised me, as she placed me down.

She turned and headed back into the house.

I was stunned that I was outside. It was as if she had heard my thoughts over time.

I had no idea the restrictions the leash put on my movement.

I sat for a moment smelling all the wonderful scents on the fresh air. I hadn't noticed the difference from inside the house, but the air seemed fresher.

Then I realized I could get to the barn where I had been dreaming about.

I glanced back at the door we had come out of, then back at the barn.

This was my chance. I instantly turned and sprinted towards the barn door.

Suddenly, I was yanked back by my neck, flipping head over paws into the air. Somehow, I managed to land on my paws completely dazed.

I was totally confused by the sudden alteration of my plans.

I sat and tugged at the line connected to the collar. Finally convinced that I could go no farther, I lay down to watch the barnyard. So close, yet so far.

Every day, rain or shine, I would meow and rub anybody and everybody's leg to get put outside.

I wasn't satisfied with lying in the windowsill anymore, now that I could be outside, closer to the barn.

Every morning, I would greet Mr. Branch as he headed out to the barn to do his chores, but he never allowed me to follow him to the barn.

Finally, one morning, I decided to go to the barn too.

Meeting Mr. Branch at the porch door, I put my plan into motion.

"Good morning, Charlie," greeted Mr. Branch, picking me up to gently rub behind my ears.

"I'll feed you when I get back," he said as he placed me back on the floor.

I didn't want to eat and wasn't about to wait for him to come back.

I wanted to go to the barn.

Now was the time to do it.

As soon as Mr. Branch opened the screen door, I made a mad dash for the opening, squeezing through just before Mr. Branch stepped out.

"Hey Charlie! You can't come out. Charlene will never let me hear the end of it," yelled Mr. Branch.

I didn't stop until I got to the barn door. A quick glance backward at Mr. Branch running towards me was enough to know I was in trouble.

I quickly leaped toward the fence connected to the corner of the barn, ducking under the bottom strand of wire into the barnyard.

I rushed around the corner of the barn, crossing the barnyard in leaps and bounds, looking for the opening I had crawled through.

Instead, there was a wall.

Quickly turning towards the water tank, I hoped there was another way in.

I skidded to a stop just past the water tank, ears twitching, eyes darting.

No sign of Mr. Branch—yet. My heart raced.

I had to keep moving.

I glanced at the wall behind the water tank and noticed a hole.

"That is my way in."

It was a tight fit, but I made it through the hole back into the barn.

The scent of straw, hay dust, and fresh air wrapped around him like an old friend.

It was almost overwhelming—but it was right. It felt right.

I sat down on the straw, taking it all in.

An opening in the wall shifted, and Mr. Branch stepped inside, scanning the barn.

Suddenly he stopped staring right at me.

I didn't know what to do next.

Mr. Branch sighed, shaking his head with a knowing smirk. "Well, I guess you got what you wanted. But now? I'm in hot water."

Chapter Nine: Charlene's Tears

I watched as Mr. Branch turn away and leave the barn.

My heart still raced—from the sprint to beat him here, from the thrill of getting away.

Now I was alone.

I sat in the dim light, sinking into the straw, letting the scent of hay and earth settle around me. The past still clung to me like old wounds—long healed, but never truly forgotten. I remembered that first night—the pain, the fear, the uncertainty.

I had been broken. Unsure if I would wake to see another morning.

And yet, here I was. Alive. Changed.

A soft creak split the silence.

The milk-house door.

The sound rippled through the barn, stirring its quiet inhabitants. The cattle, still drowsy, moved as one—heavy bodies shifting, hooves scraping the ground, nudging each other awake. The creaking meant food. They knew that.

Light spilled through the doorway as the barn door slid open, slicing through the dim haze.

Metal clanked. Hooves shuffled. The sleepy quiet shattered as the cows surged forward, pressing into their stanchions.

Mr. Branch stood framed in the light, surveying his barn. The cattle jostled impatiently, eager for their morning feed. But I wasn't watching them anymore.

I was watching her.

Charlene stood in the open doorway; her gaze locked on me.

This wasn't the face I knew—the one that smiled when I played, the one that lit up when I curled into her arms.

Her expression was tight, her shoulders stiff. And her voice—her voice was wrong.

"Charlie!"

Sharp. Hurt.

"What are you doing? You're a house cat."

I stayed frozen in place, watching as she strode forward.

She bent between the metal bars, stepping closer.

"Honey, you can't go in there with your school clothes on," Mr. Branch called gently.

"But Dad! I have to get him back into the house."

Her voice cracked. Her frustration wasn't just annoyance—it was betrayal.

"I don't disagree," Mr. Branch said, "but you're not dressed for farm work."

Charlene stepped back, exhaling hard, frustration pouring out like steam from a kettle.

Then it came.

"Charlie—you've made me mad."

Her voice wavered, but the words landed like stones.

"All this time—I took care of you. I helped you heal. I played with you. It was just you and me!"

She wiped at her eyes. The anger softened, but the hurt stayed.

"I can't believe you would just run away."

Her breath hitched.

"What if I can't find you the next time you get hurt?"

I shrank back, pressing into the straw, my instincts screaming hide. But there was nowhere to go.

"I hear the bus coming," Mr. Branch murmured, glancing toward the farmhouse.

Charlene didn't move.

"What am I supposed to do, Dad?" she whispered, voice breaking.

Then, suddenly, she ran to him, burying herself in his chest.

I watched, ears flat, tail curled tight against my body.

She cried into his shirt as he wiped her face with a cloth from his pocket.

Before I could move—before I could even understand what I had done—she turned.

She looked back at me once.

Then she was gone.

Mr. Branch followed her out, leaving me alone.

I didn't understand her anger, but I felt it—sharp, cutting, heavier than I expected.

I had never seen her cry like that. Never felt her words burn like they did now.

I didn't mean to leave her.

I just wanted what had always been mine—freedom.

Why couldn't she see that?

Why couldn't I be hers and still belong to the barn?

I sat in the barn, lost in thought.

The milk-house door creaked again—Mr. Branch was back.

This gentle creaking echoed through the barn, causing the barn life to stir again.

I watched as all the cattle moved as one, as if tied together by a puppeteer's strings. They stumbled to their hooves, their massive bodies shifting in unison.

I'm guessing they really hoped to get food this time.

My confrontation with Charlene had messed up the normal rhythm of the morning for them.

Mr. Branch stood framed in the doorway, his gaze sweeping over the barn.

It was obvious they knew his presence meant food.

They pushed and shoved for the best feeding position in the stanchions. The stanchions rattled with every shove, a percussion line under their hunger.

I stayed still, the straw warm beneath me. Something was shifting inside—not escape. Something closer to peace.

Chapter Ten:
Among the Cattle and the Goat

I watched, silent. No fear, no tension—just calm.

This wasn't an escape. It was belonging.

I watched as Mr. Branch started pouring feed from a bucket he carried.

He didn't look at me, but he started speaking as he worked. "Charlie, you broke that little girl's heart coming out here."

I heard the bucket scratch the hard surface and settle as he put it down.

He leaned on top of the stanchions, looking right at me. I couldn't tell if he was mad, too. But his calm manner and steady voice told me I wasn't in trouble.

"When you didn't go with her... I figured maybe you had your own plan. Maybe this is where you're meant to be," said Mr. Branch. "I get the impression you aren't leaving. You just wanted to be out here."

Mr. Branch instructed. "You follow me this morning, and I'll introduce you to the crew."

"These are my Angus cattle. Mrs. Flower has a nice bull calf, I named Junior. This young fellow right here in front of us is Junior."

"He always licks the trough clean."

Junior glanced at me with big eyes, a huge tongue licking his lips. I wasn't sure if he liked me—or mistook me for something snack-sized.

I stood and walked over to Mr. Branch. I curled around his legs, pressing my side into his boot.

I didn't have the words, but I hoped he could feel my thank you in the way I moved. I knew Charlene didn't understand. Not yet.

But maybe, if she could see what this place meant to me—the rhythm, the breath of it—maybe then she wouldn't feel like I'd chosen it instead of her.

Mr. Branch gave a small nod, like he'd heard my thank you without needing words. Junior snorted once, then turned back to his feed, content.

The barn was quiet except for the soft shuffle of hooves and the creak of old wood. I followed Mr. Branch as he moved deeper into the barn, past the stanchions, he pushed a wooden door open. We walked into a smaller section of the barn. It smelled of old wood, dust, hay, straw mingled together and a very strong animal scent that wasn't like Junior. There were bales stacked against the wall. My instincts told me to get higher. I dashed up a few bales, so I was almost as tall as Mr. Branch. I looked up to see nothing over me until the very top of the barn.

When I scanned the room in front of me I saw two massive shapes that stood inside a wooden box.

"I will let you girls out to romp after the sun warms the air a little," Mr. Branch promised. I ran down the bales and jumped to the floor to walk behind him. It looked like we were heading back to see Junior. I glanced to my right to see a large section of the barn that was empty but open all the way to the roof of the barn. I could see the hay stacked on the floor above. I reminded myself to check out the hay loft later.

Mr. Branch stopped and stepped through a stanchion banging the metal like the cattle did.

"Oh no, Peanut heard that for sure," whispered Mr. Branch.

"Hey, Hey, is there anybody out there," a voice bleated loudly.

I was shocked to hear the voice. I glanced around looking for the bleating sound. It appeared to be coming from a wall.

"Please, anybody. Mr. Branch can you hear me?"

"Charlie, that noise is our pygmy goat, Peanut"

"She can really make a loud racket when she starts her bleating."

I knew right away Mr. Branch didn't understand what Peanut was saying. Only I did. I was excited to meet this goat!

This side of the stalls looked like the other side where the cattle lived, but it was empty. We were walking towards another pen, but it had wood lining the walls on the inside. Mr. Branch reached a gate and opened it.

Inside, a gray-and-black goat not much bigger than me stood in the middle of the pen, staring right at the gate like he'd been waiting all morning.

"Hey Peanut," says, Mr. Branch, reaching out to rub the goat's head.

I was shocked—not at his size or color, but at how calm he looked, like he belonged there. Mr. Branch had even lined the pen with wooden panels so Peanut wouldn't slip through the gaps.

"Why am I always the last one you come to visit?" questioned Peanut.

"I know you're hungry," answered Mr. Branch.

I just laughed, because Mr. Branch did not answer Peanut's question.

"Hi, Peanut, they've been calling me Charlie," I said.

Peanut looked around Mr. Branch's leg to look at me. I smiled the best smile I could to show I was friendly. I watched as he tilted his head to get a better view.

Then, to my surprise, he dashed around Mr. Branch and bounded toward me. It wasn't really a run—more like bouncing and hopping. I could tell he was excited, but I was confused by his intentions. Before I knew what was happening, he lowered his head and butted mine. The tap knocked me backwards, rolling me onto my side. I lay there in shock and shook my head to clear the blast of pain. "Ouch! Why did you do that?" I asked.

"I'm so sorry, I was excited that you spoke to me!" gushed Peanut.

"Peanut! That wasn't nice. Are you okay Charlie?" Mr. Branch asked, as he reached down to pick me up.

I purred as he rubbed my head as if he was trying to help the pain go away. It did work, so I was grateful for the rubbing.

"You two behave while I get Peanut some pellets," said Mr. Branch, as he walked to a corner with bags.

"He really doesn't understand when I talk to him, does he?" stated Peanut.

"No, He makes good guesses at what we want or need, but truly understand, nope." answered Charlie.

"Will you be my friend?" asks Peanut.

"I think we are off to a good start, except you banging me on the head." agreed Charlie.

"Ah, that is kind of how I greet everybody. But you are the only one I've met so far," explained Peanut.

"I can hear other animals moving around, eating, talking, but nobody ever answers me."

We both turn towards the sound of pellets being dropped into a feeder.

"Ok, Peanut, you are fed. You've got clean water, and I see some hay over there in the corner. So, you are all set." explained Mr. Branch.

"Come on Charlie," Mr. Brach calls, as he heads for the gate.

I start following without thinking to say goodbye.

"Hey, what about me?" bleats Peanut.

I think he's asking me the question, I answer, "I'll come back to chat."

"Peanut! You know I can't let you run around the barn. You had the cattle all irritated the last time you got loose," Mr. Branch answers over his shoulder as he steps out of the gate. "Hurry Charlie, I need to get this closed."

I scamper out of the gate just as Mr. Branch swings it shut on Peanut rushing towards the gate.

"Sorry Peanut, maybe when Charlene gets home from school I will let you out for a little while," promises Mr. Branch.

"Bye Peanut," I yell. "I will come back to see you in a little bit."

He stood at the gate, ears drooping. "Somebody better come back. It gets really quiet in here."

"I will," I said. "I know what quiet feels like too."

Chapter Eleven:
Welcome to the Barn Family

I followed Mr. Branch back to the stanchions as he bent down to step through.

Mr. Branch stopped and looked down at me. "Charlie, we are done with chores and introductions," stated Mr. Branch.

"This day did not start well. First, you tricked me into leaving the house and reaching the barn."

I slowly lowered my body to the cement. I wrapped my tail around my paws with my tail slowly twitching close to my right fore paw. I could tell he wasn't happy, but he wasn't mad like Charlene had been.

"Second, you broke Charlene's heart. She believed you'd be her house cat, her companion. But you seem very comfortable in this barn. I don't know where you came from, but I'm betting you had to fend for yourself."

I glanced to my left to see Junior staring wide-eyed at Mr. Branch. I guess he'd never heard Mr. Branch talk in such a tone before.

"Lastly, welcome to the barn. I'm hoping you are a good mouser. They're turning my feed into a mouse buffet," he said very calmly.

I watched as Mr. Branch turned, walked out the milk-house door, and slid it closed. Then I heard the barn door close as he left.

"Wow, that was a lot," whispered Junior.

I stayed crouched, still staring at the milk-house door. "Yeah, I agree. I made a decision this morning that changed a lot of things," I said quietly, my mind flashing through the day so far.

I heard the call of birds high in the rafters of the barn. The scent of animals, straw, dust, and feed settled over me like a cloud. These weren't the soft, sweet smells of Charlene's room—her warmth, her clean world. The smells and warmth of my guardian, friend.

"What do you mean by changed? Nothing changed for me," Junior says, a little confused. "Well, it did change a little, because you came in through the hole in the wall and Mr. Branch found you. Then he left. Which means our feeding time was messed up. "Wait, then Charlene came in and was really mad at you," said Junior. "I was trying to hide behind my mother, because I thought she was mad at me. I was kind of glad to realize it wasn't me in trouble, but you."

I sigh, as I push myself into a sitting position and turn towards Junior.

"Yes, she was mad at me," I agreed.

"But honestly, I don't understand why. I'm still her friend or at least I think I am," I said, defending myself—but mostly trying to make sense of it out loud.

"I was hurt and had crawled into the barn for shelter. She found me and got me help. Then took care of me, herself, for weeks. She will always be my friend!" My voice came out stronger than I expected.

"Well, I was born here. Mom takes care of me, but Mr. Branch always takes care of us," said Junior. "I will always consider him our friend because he feeds us."

The image of Junior in Mr. Branch's house made me laugh out loud. "I can tell Mr. Branch loves his barn family," said Charlie, still giggling.

Mrs. Flower's gentle voice added, "Hmm, it seems you may be confused with the bond between family and friend." "Mr. Branch is part of our barn family because he protects, heals, feeds, and provides shelter for us."

"On the other hand, Charlene is our friend, a sweet girl. She comes by, says hi. Gives us a rub, hay, or water when she sees we need it."

"It sounds to me like Charlene was your family. She provided you shelter, feed, protection, and healing," states Mrs. Flower, defining Charlene's position in Charlie's life.

"But..." she exhaled slowly. "Then you up and left her—and everything she meant to you—to make your own choice."

"I've always been on my own," I started, but—

"Oh no, I don't need you to explain your feelings to me," Mrs. Flower stopped him.

"Our barn family is made up of many individuals working together for the farm. You are now one of us, Mr. Branch said so," states Mrs. Flower. "I have no idea what a barn cat can do for me, but I'm assuming you are a good one to keep an eye on Junior for me. I also hope you can figure out that tiny little goat. Charlene is your problem to handle," states Mrs. Flower.

I looked at Mrs. Flower's face. There was no anger or judging, just straight out telling me where I fit in the barn.

"Mrs. Flower, I promise to be a full working member of this barn family. Peanut has already told me he needs a friend. I will be that for him and Junior. I will protect them as best as I can." I started with earnest, sitting a little straighter to make myself look stronger.

"At the same time, I have to fix the mess I made with Charlene," I whispered.

The barn was quiet again. I listened to the soft scrape of hooves in straw, and for the first time, I felt like the day was mine to repair.

Chapter Twelve :
Doors Opening, Bonds Forming

I was alerted to Mr. Branch returning, by the squeak of the metal hinges on the barn door. Then the milk-house door slid open.

It was funny that nobody jumped up to greet Mr. Branch. I could hear soft snorts from sleepy cows shifting in straw, others settled down on the straw to chew some hay. Even Junior made no move to get up.

Then Peanut started his bleating,"Hey don't forget me. I'm ready to get out and roam the barn."

I looked at Mr. Branch with his stone-faced expression. Slowly changed to a grin and shake his head. "Peanut, you know you are the last animal I will let out."

He opened a gate into the cattle stalls. A distinct metallic clank rang as Mr. Branch closes the gate behind him. As he stepped into the straw all the cattle stood up.

"It's about time you opened our door Mr. Branch," mooed Mrs. Flower. "We all could use some fresh air. Come on ladies,"

All the cattle started moving towards Mr. Branch anticipating the door sliding open.

"Alright ladies, I've got to slide the door open first. Give me just a second." Mr. Branch told the gathering cows.

As the big doors opened, a ribbon of sunlight stretched across the floor as the doors parted, warming the straw in golden patches. Sounds of birds fluttering, calling from the rafters. A breeze carried in the sharp green scent of pasture grass, lifting the warm musk of straw and animal from the barn floor. Mrs. Flower was the first one out.

"Ah, that fresh air and smell of the pasture is wonderful. It was getting a little stuffy in there this morning," called Mrs. Flower, just speaking her thoughts to everybody.

I watched as Junior danced out the door behind all the cows.

"Come on Charlie," Junior called. We can play in the dirt of the barnyard or go to the pasture," he said, looking at me with a mischievous grin.

"In a second, Mr. Branch is heading to the horses. I need to follow him first," I yelled, as I trotted towards Mr. Branch to catch up.

Mr. Branch had already slid the door open to the horse area. I trotted in and ran up the bales, my paws thudded softly across the hay, the edges prickling underfoot before I sat with my tail curled around my paws watching Mr. Branch work.

"Ms. Anne and Ms. Dolly, I'm going to slide the north door open. That gives you a small pasture to yourself this afternoon," Mr. Branch explained with his back to the horses.

I heard the low creak of wood as Ms. Dolly leans against the stall. Both ladies neighed their approval to Mr. Branch.

"I prefer that pasture most days. Sometimes the cows can really chatter about nothing at all," neighed Ms. Anne.

"Absolutely," agreed Ms. Dolly.

Mr. Branch had opened a sliding door to the pasture. I could see that the fencing faced towards the black path with an open field on the other side. It seemed so long ago that I was out there fending for myself.

I watched as Mr. Branch slid open the wall in front of Ms. Dolly. He then reached as high as he could to connect a rope to this thing she wore on her head. He guided her to the door and outside before stopping her to take off the rope. He then turned around to get Ms. Anne, repeating the same steps.

"Ok, Ms. Anne you girls relax and enjoy the pasture," he said, as he patted her hip and walked back to hang up the rope.

As he walked towards the cattle door, he stopped and closed a gate that blocked off the big area with hay.

"Hmm, I guess he doesn't want the horses over there," I thought.

"Charlie, hurry! I need to close this door,"Mr. Branch instructed.

I dashed down the bales and through the door and stopped about half-way down the walkway and turned to see what was next.

Peanut hadn't stopped bleating the whole time Mr. Branch was opening doors and letting everybody out.

Mr. Branch turned and looked right at me.

"Ok Charlie, this is a big test. I'm going to let Peanut out. He cannot leave the dirt of the barnyard, and he must stay inside the fencing," instructed Mr. Branch.

It seemed like a lot to ask of me... but I stood up, tail flicking. "I've got this," I tried to say without words.

He bent low to step through the stanchions, and I followed him with a few leaps. He walked straight to the gate on Peanut's pen. As he started opening the pen Peanut became quiet.

Mr. Branch opened the gate, knelt down quickly to catch the goat barreling toward the opening.

"Ha, ha, nice try Peanut,"Mr. Branch laughed, as he stood holding the little goat close to his chest.

He turned and started walking towards the big opening to the barnyard, talking to Peanut the whole way.

"Peanut, I made Charlie your guardian. I've already told him your limits. You better behave," chided Mr. Branch. "Mrs. Branch keeps telling me to make a separate goat pen, but I'm really hoping I don't have to."

Mr. Branch stopped in the middle of the barnyard dirt and placed Peanut on the ground.

Peanut immediately started hopping and spinning with joy.

Mr. Branch just turned towards the barn, "Good luck, Charlie!"

"Yahoo!" yelled Peanut, as he bounced around in circles. "I get so bored inside my pen. It's really nice out here."

"Ah, who are you?" asks Junior. "You're so tiny."

I took it upon myself to make the introductions. "Junior meet Peanut. Peanut meet Junior." "You two have never met in the barn?" I asked, confused.

"Ah, no," Peanut says slowly.

"I've only seen our family group and Ms. Anne and Ms. Dolly," stated Junior.

"Are you the voice we hear screaming at Mr. Branch every morning?" Junior asks, quizzically.

"Well, I have to get his attention," Peanut said, meekly.

"Wait, you two have never really met? How is that possible? You live in the barn together?" wonders Charlie. "Your family, right" I ask, confused.

"Family?" says Peanut, twisting his head side to side.

"Hmm, Family. I never thought of family beyond my mom," states Junior.

"Yea, but the barn is safety, food, a connection for all of us," I state. "That would make us a barn family."

"I don't know. That is a lot to think about," says Junior, shaking his head.

"I agree. I mean, I don't even have friends and I'm part of a barn family?" doubts Peanut.

I jump up onto the edge of the water tank, my paws slipping and sliding as I try to balance on the edge of the tank, almost falling in for a swim. I finally settle on the edge in a precarious position for a drink. I can see the bottom of the tank through the water.

"What are you doing, Charlie?" asked Junior, cocking his head trying to see into the tank.

"I'm getting a drink of water," purred I.

"Water? What's water?" asked Junior.

"Mr. Branch pours water into a container in my pen every day," states Peanut.

Looking confused, Junior responded, "Really?"

I lean down to the surface and gently lapped some water to quench my thirst before answering Junior.

"What does it look like?" asks Junior.

I lean back to answer Junior's question, when he jumps. Stretching upward, he teetered on his hind legs, his forelegs scrabbling for a hold on the tank's rim. His chest thumped against the edge as he hoisted himself up.

"What are you doing?" I ask.

"I'm just curious," answers Junior.

"Hey, it's no fair. I can't jump that high," whines Peanut.

I'm comfortably balanced on the edge of the tank watching Junior's eyes. I can tell he's thinking. He's looking curiously at the shimmering surface of the water. It was still and clear, almost like a sheet of ice. I gently flicked my tail waiting to see what Junior will do.

The mysterious liquid seemed to call to Junior.

I watched him, a sly grin playing on his face. "Careful, Junior," I teased, tone laced with a hint of mischief. "You might see something you don't want to."

Junior craned his neck, his nose hovering closer and closer to the surface.

"I can't tell what it smells like," states Junior. "It doesn't look like much," he muttered, squinting. Suddenly, he pushes with his back legs, he dipped his muzzle into the cool liquid.

For a moment, everything was quiet. Too quiet.

Then Junior explodes out of the water, with a sputtering noise, his ears flattening against his head. Water sprayed in every direction, droplets catching the sunlight as I'm showered with water.

Junior had jumped down from the edge of the tank shaking his head furiously, to clear the water out of his nostrils, coughing and blowing his muzzle the whole time.

I jumped back, narrowly dodging the most of the spray of water erupting from Junior's flailing muzzle.

My fur bristled as the droplets glistened on my coat. "Junior!" I yowled, shaking a paw in mock frustration, though the corner of my mouth twitched into a reluctant grin.

"Junior! Stop shaking water everywhere!" yells Peanut, dancing and dodging water drops.

I could hear a deep rumble of laughter coming from Junior.

My paws started to slip on the edge of the tank, sliding on the water Junior had tossed around.

I growled low, glaring at Junior's amused face, but my indignation made my footing increasingly precarious. I wobbled as my claws scratched the tank's slippery surface, my balance teetering on the edge. "Junior, stop laughing! You're distracting—"

Then out of the corner of my eye, I see a small flash of black and gray running head long towards the tank.

There was a hard smack on the tank, I watched the water vibrate in the tank, I felt a slight tremble on the wall I was wobbling on.

I give a sharp yelp, as I lose my balance completely. Time seemed to slow as my legs flailed in the air, my tail whipping like a panicked banner behind me. My expression froze in a wide-eyed mix of terror and disbelief.

I could see Junior froze mid-shake, his mouth hanging open, eyes widening as he watched my fate unfolding in slow motion.

My yowl echoed through the barnyard, accompanied by the sound of amused clucking from the chickens somewhere nearby.

Climbing out of the tank, hissing in disgust at getting wet, I hopped to the ground shaking furiously trying to dry off.

Junior's laughter started as a rumble deep in his chest, before bursting out uncontrollably.

"Ha, you're all wet, Charlie," laughed Junior, as he rolled in the dirt on his back.

"It's not funny, water is to drink not to swim in," I scolded, quite upset about getting wet.

"But you look so funny all wet," giggled Peanut.

"You sticking your muzzle in the water was funny. Getting all wet is disgusting," I replied, flinging water off my paw.

The sun had climbed higher, and the laughter had settled into slower breaths. My fur was nearly dry.

That's when Mrs. Flower's voice floated over the fence.

"Junior," called Mrs. Flower. "Time to come join us, the clover's just right."

Junior stilled. "Coming, Mama!" he said, then nudged me with his nose. "Charlie, watch Peanut. He'll try to follow me—I just know it."

Chapter Thirteen: Adventures with Peanut

"Let's go with Junior," says Peanut, bouncing around me.

The memory of that attack flickering behind my eyes. "I'm not ready to go too far from the barn," I admitted. "It's...safe."

"But we'll stick together; we'll make sure we have fun together." I thought of how small we both were, and how my siblings got carried off by that flying hunter. Yes, better to be safe and have fun together.

"Fine," said Peanut, perking up. "What should we do?"

"How about we go visit Ms. Anne and Ms. Dolly in the small pasture? I can see the horses in the smaller front pasture. It looks like we can just duck under the fence wire and be in the pasture."

"I'm with you," agreed Peanut.

So, I lead the way.

Since the horses were standing in the far corner nibbling at the grass, I adjusted our path to stay in their line of sight. The last thing I wanted was to startle Ms. Anne—or worse, Ms. Dolly. Big hooves and surprise don't mix.

"Charlie, good to see you." Ms. Anne mumbled between nibbles, as she kept moving a step at a time.

"Who is that with you?" asked Ms. Dolly, standing chewing, staring at Peanut.

"Ms. Dolly and Ms. Anne, this is Peanut," I introduce them.

"Is it your brother? You don't look the same," asks Ms Dolly.

"Oh, no ma'am," Charlie answered. "Mr. Branch called him a pygmy goat. Yet the idea that he could be his brother was enticing.

"Yes, I'm on the cattle side in a pen by myself," explained Peanut

"Are you two out getting into mischief today?" asked Ms. Anne.

"Uhhh, no ma'am. Uhh, well may be a little," I stammered.

Ms. Dolly let out a dramatic sigh, flicking her tail in annoyance. "Oh, just wonderful, it's starting to get a little warm out here. Now I get to roast in the sun."

"We can stand in the cool barn shadow, but the grass is getting thin over there." answers Ms. Anne, still walking and nibbling.

"At least we don't have to listen to Mrs. Flower jabber about Junior," Ms. Anne huffed.

"Oh, definitely, that cow can go on about nothing forever," chimed Ms. Dolly.

"The clover in the pasture would taste good, though," said Ms. Anne, staring longingly across the fence at the clover on the other side.

"Yes, but remember that snake," Ms. Dolly reminded her.

"What snake?" I asked, lying in the grass next to Peanut.

"Oh, it was nothing," brushed off Ms. Ann. "I was out in the pasture last summer when something in the clover startled me," she began.

"If she hadn't jumped and stomped that snake into the ground, you'd never know what could have happened," finished Ms. Dolly.

I sat up immediately, my full attention on Ms. Anne. "You stomped a snake?" I echoed in disbelief. Then, tilting my head, I added, "Wait... what's a snake?"

Ms. Dolly huffed, flicking her tail. "Don't be ridiculous, Charlie," she muttered, exasperated.

"Now, be nice, he is still young," Ms. Ann reminded Ms. Dolly.

"Snakes are disgusting, slithering, creepy creatures that live in the hedgerow between the pasture and the cornfield," she explained with a shudder.

"How could something in the grass bother you?" It made no sense to me.

"Snakes are hard to see as they slither in the tall grass. Which spooks us and we just stomped naturally," answered Ms. Anne.

"A bite from a snake can make us very sick. In our condition, we can't afford to be sick," explained Ms. Anne.

"Mostly, rattlers and copperheads are our worst enemies," continued Ms. Dolly.

Dangerous predators here? In the grass? I shivered, remembering the fox attack, and the birds that swooped up my brother. Could I be in as much danger here as out there? After what I'd just told Peanut? I wanted to ask more about snakes, but Ms. Anne changed the topic.

"I'm a little hungry," said Ms. Anne as she wandered out into the grass, nibbling as she walked.

Ms. Dolly turned to join Ms. Anne.

"We'll see you later, Charlie. Nice to meet you Peanut!"

And then it was just me and Peanut.

Chapter Fourteen: The Distance Between Us

As the horses wandered towards the other pasture, my ears twitched at the low growl of the bus engine on the black path. I sprang to my paws, heart already racing. I spun toward the black path—same bus as this morning; I was sure of it.

I leapt into a sprint toward the barnyard, yelling, "Peanut, we need to run to the barnyard!"

"Why are we running to the barnyard?" yelled Peanut, right behind me.

"Charlene is coming home," I answered, sucking air as I run.

I skidded into the barnyard, tail curling tightly around my paws, chest rising and falling as I watched the road.

Peanut trotted toward the fence, curiosity bouncing in every step.

Charlene's two friends stepped off first. Then Charlene—last. Her gaze swept across the fence—met mine—and moved on. My breath hitched. Did she see me?

"That's Charlie!" Indiana beamed.

"Oh my gosh, the little goat is adorable," Scout squealed.

"That's our pygmy goat named Peanut," Charlene answered, catching up with Scout and ignoring me.

"That is Charlie!" exclaimed Indiana. "Hey Charlie, what are you doing over there?"

Charlene rushed ahead. "Hey, we are really on a tight time schedule. Your mom will be here in 45 minutes."

"Come on Indiana, she's right. Mom will be here soon," agreed Scout, then turned towards the house.

My heart sunk in my chest as I watched Charlene turn around with her friends. I was sure she looked at me, but then she ignored me. I guess she was still mad at me for running to the barn this morning. But I wasn't sure why. She could easily come to the barn, right? She could see me anytime she wanted.

"Charlie, that was so cool! I've never met Charlene's friends before, "chattered Peanut excitedly.

"Ah, yea. Her friends are nice. I met them when Charlene was taking care of me," I whispered with disappointment.

"Charlene rubs my head sometimes, but I don't think she considers me a friend," Peanut stated, with wide-eyed awe.

"I think I may have lost my friend," Charlie murmured, more to the dust at his paws than to Peanut.

"Here cows! Here cows," yelled Mr. Branch, shaking a bucket with some feed in it.

Peanut and I both jumped, totally surprised he was standing in the barnyard.

"Come on girls!" he calls again.

I looked towards the pasture and saw Mrs. Flower leading the cows towards the barn. I think about the snake the horse told us about. Were snakes a problem for the cows, too? I make a mental note to talk to Mrs. Flower this evening.

"Ms. Anne, Ms. Dolly, come on girls," he yells, shaking the bucket again. Then turns towards the barn door.

Peanut and I watched as the parade of cows were all in line behind Mrs. Flower, heading to the barn door. Junior was the last one in line. I'd not see Ms. Anne or Ms. Dolly, but I heard the clip-clop of their hooves coming from the horse manger. Everybody is inside but us.

"Come on, Peanut, or we will miss dinner," I suggest, looking at Peanut with a smile.

"But that means I'm back in my pen. Alone."

"You're not alone. We're all inside," I try to comfort him.

"It's not the same."

I went to argue with him, but then I realized I was all alone now, too. I obviously couldn't go back to Charlene's bed, where I'd been sleeping this whole time. The thought saddened me, but then I reminded myself I made my choice. I now had my freedom.

"Peanut, how about me sharing your pen with you tonight?" I said, smiling at my friend.

"That would be awesome! Thank you," Peanut said, very excited about me sleeping in the pen.

"I have to chat with Mrs. Flower first," I explained. "But then I will be in your pen, promise."

"Come on, Peanut. We need to get you in the pen," calls Mr. Branch, stepping through the stanchions.

I head towards my new bowl, wondering what Charlene is going to do with my old one. Then I see Charlene's bowl for me sitting on the walkway.

I sit down in front of the bowl, not feeling hunger. Sadness hangs heavily on my shoulders. I hadn't known that me wanting to be free in the barn meant I'd never be friends with Charlene again.

I heard the stanchions clang, boots scraping the walkway, as if they're coming towards me.

"Well, Charlie, it's been a long day," Mr. Branch started. "I appreciate you keeping an eye on Peanut. This is the first time he's actually stayed in the barnyard. I told Charlene you just wanted to be part of the barn family," he said, kneeling to check a latch. "You proved me right by not running off."

He nodded at the bowl. "She said you needed your feed bowl, or you wouldn't eat."

I was stunned. Charlene actually thought about me, even though she wouldn't look at me.

"Good night, Charlie. Sleep well," Mr. Branch turned and left the barn, closing the doors behind him.

Chapter Fifteen: New Friends, Old Tensions

The barn was still. I sat where the light faded, staring at the old feed bowl Charlene had picked out just for me.

Mr. Branch had filled it. But I remembered when Charlene fed me—it held bits of turkey or tuna, or whatever Charlene had scraped together after sneaking it off the kitchen counter. I remembered the warmth of her lap, her fingers tracing lazy spirals behind my ear, the way she'd whisper secrets into my fur like I was her diary.

Now it's just a bowl.

I've made friends here. A pact with Peanut. Trust from Junior. Mrs. Flower's soft wisdom. Even Mr. Branch's gruff kindness.

But—I didn't know I'd have to trade Charlene.

My stomach clenched. I looked at the bowl. I didn't feel hunger—only hollow.

Cows shifted and sighed into their favorite spots, the rustle of hay like a lullaby under their hooves. Mrs. Flower eased down first, curling her legs beneath her. The others followed, one by one, folding into the warmth of each other's company like a woven quilt of breath and fur and trust.

But Junior—he lay alone.

Tucked close to the horse manger wall, his back to the rest of the herd. His tail flicked once, then stilled. I watched him from the walkway, my ears flicking at the soft creak of rafters overhead.

He didn't look sad. Just... separate.

And that's when it hit me: Even surrounded by family, you can still feel alone.

I gave myself a good shake. No more of that. I had better things to do—like find out how safe the pasture really was.

I padded softly across the barn, weaving through the sleepy murmurs of cows and the rustle of settling hooves. The air smelled of hay and dust and comfort. Just ahead, Mrs. Flower was settling into her corner, her eyes half-lidded but alert. Her ears flicked as I approached.

"Mrs. Flower," I whispered, trying not to startle her, "can I talk to you about... something in the pasture?"

She blinked once—slow and steady—then adjusted her legs beneath her with a soft sigh. "Of course, Charlie," she said, her voice low and warm. "Come, curl up close so we don't wake the others."

I stepped gently through the straw and settled beside her.

"There's something... the horses said today," I began. "Ms. Anne and Ms. Dolly—they talked about a snake in the pasture. Said it slithered through the clover last summer, near where Junior plays."

Mrs. Flower didn't move, but I felt the weight of her listening.

"They said it could be dangerous. Rattlers. Copperheads. I guess I just—what if it comes back? What if we can't see it?"

She was quiet for a long time, and I wondered if I'd made a mistake asking her. It showed her I was afraid. Then:

"Snakes are part of the land," she murmured, "same as the grass and the wind. Most want nothing to do with us. But you're right to be cautious, especially with young ones like Junior."

Her ear flicked toward the other cows. "That's why we stay close. We watch the ground and each other. If something shifts in the grass, we move slow. We listen."

I nodded, though my chest still felt tight.

Mrs. Flower turned her head slightly and nuzzled the back of my ear. "Thank you for caring, Charlie. That makes you part of the herd, too."

I thought about the barn. The pasture, vast and open, felt like a world I wasn't ready to trust. I hadn't yet ventured past the barnyard fence into the cattle pasture, but the tree line blurred in my vision as memories clawed at the edges of my mind—shadows, sharp teeth, the chilling fear of a fight he barely escaped. My experience with the outside world had cured me of wandering. The world could be very unfriendly at times and downright cruel when it wanted to be. Even if Charlene was mad at me, I was lucky to have found my way here.

Chapter Sixteen:
The Meaning of Family

I left Mrs. Flower still worried about snakes. Even more since she said I was "part of the herd." I know she was labeling me as Junior's protector. I don't mind, I like Junior, but he goes to the cattle pasture.

I've never been there. Knowing snakes are out there, I don't want to go. Should I stop the others from going, too? Mrs. Flower didn't seem too concerned, but what if she was being too optimistic?

I weaved my way through the black mounds scattered across the straw in all stages of sleep.

I danced through the stanchions, heading towards Peanut's pen. The gate is locked, but I'm sure I can get over the top.

I run and leap, landing on the first box, immediately springing to the second box, and leap over the pen's side. Landing in the straw with Peanut staring right at me.

"I wish I could do that!" yells Peanut excitedly.

"Shh...not so loud. Everybody is trying to sleep." I try to calm him down.

"Where do I bed down?"

"If it was cold, Mr. Branch would turn on my lamp and I'd sleep there," explains Peanut. "But tonight feels good, not too hot, not too cold. So, I just kick some straw into a pile. Then just snuggle into until I'm comfortable."

I noticed a snuggle hole in the straw. I'm sure it will be warm, but not as warm as Charlene's bed cover.

My head is closer to Peanut. I tuck in my legs and curl my tail around my legs like a blanket.

I was restless. I had too much weighing on my mind—Charlene, snakes, the barnyard... fun with Peanut felt distant, almost unreachable.

As my eyelids grew heavy, the warmth of the barn surrounded me, pulling me into restless dreams. The dreams were not peaceful—snakes slithered in my thoughts, twisting them into terror. I envisioned a snake being as tall as a tree with four paws as big as Ms. Ann's hoof and claws that could do terrible damage. Their mouths filled with huge, pointed teeth.

I dreamed of going to the pasture to get Junior, when suddenly this snake appeared out of nowhere. I cowered in fear as I looked up at this disgusting creature. The creature towered above me and Junior, drooling and snarling at us. With a guttural snarl, the beast lunged—its enormous claws flashing through the air, slicing toward me and Junior as the nightmare swallowed me whole. The air stank of rot and fear as its shadow blotted out the sky.

I woke with a jolt to find myself standing up with every hair on my body on end and my heart pounding madly, staring into the darkness.

"It's just a dream," I whispered, but the words felt hollow. My skin still crawled, my muscles still tense, as if the nightmare hadn't fully released me.

Suddenly, a shiver raced up my spine, causing me to shake as if I were cold. "At least I hope it was a bad dream."

Chapter Seventeen: Charlene's Silence

I heard the telltale sounds of Mr. Branch entering the barn, squeaking hinges, scuff of boots on the hard floor, and the door sliding open. I realized it must be morning feeding time. My dreams were so vivid. I still felt tired from the struggles in my mind.

I stand and stretch from head to tail. I give myself a good shake to dust off my coat of any stray straw sticking to me.

I looked at Peanut, still tucked in his snuggle hole. I can tell by his light breathing that he's still sleeping. I decided not to wake him just yet.

I sprang to the top of the board wall, landing in silence, then hopped down the stack of boxes, retracing the path I'd taken the night before.

Ahead, I saw Junior—not on his hay, but standing in the middle of the runway, directly in Mr. Branch's line of sight.

Junior jerked upright as if stung. His hooves clacked wildly against the smooth barn floor, slipping like they'd hit ice. Then, in a full-body lurch of panic, he lunged at the stanchion gap—headfirst, bold as an arrow—but his shoulders smacked the cool metal bars with a startling crash.

He wriggled and kicked, straw flying, as the barn echoed with the clatter of desperation.

"You little rascal. You won't be able to do that much longer," chuckled Mr. Branch, a broad smile creasing his face as he walked over, his boots a steady rhythm against the hard floor.

He leaned casually against the stanchion, inspecting Junior's flailing like a man checking fence posts for cracks. I chuckled, watching as Junior tried to vanish behind Mrs. Flower's bulk. There was no fooling Mr. Branch—but in this barn, a little mischief was part of the morning routine.

"Mrs. Flower, you have one fine-looking boy there. Yes, ma'am, Junior may only be 95 pounds now, but he shows all the characteristics of easily becoming a prized 2000-pound bull when full-grown. You just keep feeding him mother's milk and he'll grow like a weed," praised Mr. Branch. "But when are you going to teach your son to stay where he belongs?" Mr. Branch chuckled.

Mrs. Flower blinked at Mr. Branch, her face showing no emotion, tail swishing lazily, as if she truly grasped Mr. Branch's question—but had no defense for Junior's antics. She swished her tail at some morning flies and stood stock still as Mr. Branch reached in and rubbed her broad head between the ears.

I caught the twinkle in his eyes. "Charlene can be just as hardheaded," he added, more to himself than to her. "So I know how it goes."

Satisfied that nothing was broken, he turned and resumed his chore routine.

"Hey, don't forget me!" Peanut's voice rang out, chipper even from inside his pen.

"Morning, Peanut," Mr. Branch called back, continuing his route with a practiced ease.

I watched as Mr. Branch disappeared into the horse manger, his boots scuffing softly against the barn floor.

I turned toward Junior, who stood nearby. "Why were you out on the walkway?" I asked.

He answered with a shrug. "I don't know. I like the cool floor sometimes."

He glanced down, his hooves shifting slightly. "Mr. Branch seems like he's in a hurry today. He didn't feed us first."

Just then, I heard the scrape of boots as Mr. Branch returned, the metal bucket swinging gently in one hand.

He tipped the last scoop of feed into the trough and gave the pail a shake. "There we go. Breakfast for everyone," he muttered, brushing his hands on his jeans.

He started for the main door; one boot planted on the threshold—then paused.

"Almost forgot—can't skip my smallest mouths."

He turned back, crossed to Peanut's pen, and poured a generous helping of pellets into the dish. Then he set down a smaller bowl beside the walkway just for me.

"There you go, Charlie," he said, flashing a quick smile. "Won't have time to open the door till I'm back, so eat up, stay cozy, and no escaping—deal?"

I twitched my ears at that last bit.

"I hate to rush off like this," he called down the barn aisle, his voice rising a little, "but I've got to get to the grain store to have our feed mix made."

He gave a final glance toward Mrs. Flower. "I'll open the barn as soon as I get back—promise. Just hang tight, girls—and boys," he added, nodding at Peanut's pen. "You've all got full bellies and clean straw. Try not to stir up too much trouble while I'm gone."

He chuckled, slid the big barn door mostly closed behind him, and latched the bolt with a solid clack.

Moments later, I heard the truck engine grumble awake. Gravel crunched beneath the tires, the sound fading as he pulled away.

And then—I heard it. Distant but rising. The growl of the school bus winding up the road.

My ears perked. My tail twitched.

I padded a few steps toward the gate, heart thudding. I told myself I just wanted to see the road. But I already knew that wasn't true.

She was coming. Charlene.

Chapter Eighteen: Night in the Barn

I was determined to see Charlene before she got on her bus. Mr. Branch just locked down the barn until he got back, but I knew I could get out.

I dashed across the straw towards the back wall that slides. In my hurry I disturbed the cows. Some jumped to their hooves, stomping and dancing away from me. I really wasn't that close to them, but they sure acted like I was. Others just huffed as I ran by.

"Charlie, what are you doing? Just lay down and relax," yelled Mrs. Flower.

Junior met me at the back wall.

"What's going on, Charlie?" Junior whispered in my face.

"I've got to get out to see Charlene this morning," I said, not stopping long enough to make eye contact. "She ignored me yesterday; I don't want her to do that again." It hurt too much, but I didn't want to get into all that with Junior.

I had used this gap to get into the barn. So, I knew I could get out.

There it is! A gap between the sliding wall and the barn wall.

I ran to the gap, stuck my head through. It was tighter than I remembered. I had to twist my shoulders a little, scraping my repaired shoulder along the barn wall as I went. There was no pain, but I remembered when there was. I had to twist to get my back legs on the sliding wall to push myself through, landing behind the water tank.

I was in the barnyard. I needed just a few seconds to sprint around the tank and head to the fence line. My paws were moving before I told them, too. I took a hard right turn to face the fence line. I'm looking at the yellow bus, when I see the house door open. I lose my footing, sliding, scrambling in the dirt. I hit my right hip, using my front paws I get righted, and my back paws launch my forward as they touch the ground. There is a clear spot with no weeds directly in front of me. I slide to a sitting stop, heart pounding, I'm sucking air as if I was chased.

I'm looking right at Charlene. Her head pops up.

She stops. She's looking right at me.

"Come on, please wave!" I think.

Without even a flicker of recognition, as if we hadn't spent all that time together, she turns toward the bus and disappears.

My breath disappears in a heavy sigh, stunned that she didn't even wave.

"I'm still here, Charlene!" I mewed as the bus passed. "Can't you come see me in the barn?"

Did I make a huge mistake by wanting to be in the barn, to come and go as I please? Should I slink back to Charlene and ask her to take me back?

To lock me up again?

I look around the farm. It seems empty. The life of the farm is still closed in the barn. I feel alone. The light breeze brings me the sound of plants waving, leaves brushing each other, and the sound of the sky hunter calling. I tremble at my stupidity.

I realize I've been sitting still in the open. Easy prey for the sky hunters.

I quickly stand and walk a few steps to the nearest portion of the barn wall. I know against the barn wall I'm protected. I glanced at the sky, but can't see the hunter.

I decided it's time to go back inside; I need to talk to Junior.

I follow the wall around towards the water tank and my getaway hole.

The sweet smell of straw, hay, and friends all mingled together seeps out of the gap to greet me.

One last look at the sky. Then I work my way back into the barn.

"Hey Charlie, you're back," Junior said, excited to see me.

It felt good to be noticed. It felt good to have somebody waiting to see me come back.

"Hi Junior." I responded, but even I can hear I lack his excitement.

"Did it work? Did she say hi?"

Feeling drained, I walked a few steps into the straw and plopped down on my side.

"What's wrong, Charlie?" Junior asked, as he laid down next to me.

He lay with his legged tucked in close to himself, more in a sitting position than a laying position. He was alert, looking at me with worried cow eyes.

That actually made me feel good.

"She saw me," I began. "She looked right at me. But she didn't wave or yell my name, nothing. Just got on the bus and left."

Junior runs his tongue over his lips, and says, "Wow, that is tough."

"Give her more time. She will come pet you," soothes Junior.

"I hope so," I mumble into the straw.

I don't want to think about Charlene anymore—or how much she hurt me—so I start talking about another one of my worries.

"Have you ever seen a snake in the pasture?" I don't want my new friends to get hurt.

"What's a snake?" questioned Junior, confused.

"I don't know exactly," I replied. "But I had a bad dream about them last night,"

"Now Charlie, let's stop this conversation right here," Mrs. Flower instructed, sternly." I don't want false fears to be created about nothing."

"Junior, I don't want you worrying about snakes." Mrs. Flower states, "You are never alone in the pasture. We all take care of each other."

"But Ms. Anne said..." I couldn't help arguing. Maybe Mrs. Flower wasn't taking the dangers of snakes seriously?

"Charlie," Mrs. Flower softened her tone. "Go talk to Mr. Combs at the chicken coop. He has to deal with snakes all the time. He'll tell you there's nothing to be afraid of."

Mr. Combs, the rooster. I haven't met him yet. Maybe Peanut could come with me. Then neither one of us would be alone while I got answers about snakes.

Chapter Nineteen: Lessons from the Herd

I watched Mr. Branch work on opening Peanut's pen. The rattling of the gate, thumping of the wood. Mr. Branch knelt before opening the gate.

I watched as he swung the gate slowly open, waiting for Peanut to charge. I could tell the gate was open, but nothing happened.

Mr. Branch stands up, looking down into the pen.

"Peanut, what is going on? You didn't charge the gate," said Mr. Branch, sounding confused. "You spend a day with Charlie playing outside and you are a changed goat?"

He changes position to one side of the gate.

Out walks Peanut.

"Charlie, I don't know what you did, but keep doing it," praises Mr. Branch with a big smile.

I join Peanut and we slowly walk to the open door to the barnyard.

I whisper, "What is going on?"

Peanut smiles at me. "I'm just controlling my energy until we get outside in the sun," he whispers. "Walk fast. I'm ready to burst out and kick my heels."

We walk stride for stride next to each other, heading for the sunlight.

We stop right at the edge of the barn where the shade ends and sunlight begins.

We look at each other. A grin creeps up our face. I wink at Peanut.

"Let's go," I yell, dashing out the door into the warmth of the sun.

Peanut is a streak across the dirt. He stops about midway to the grassy edge and starts hopping in a circle.

"We're outside!" he screams.

I realize the emptiness I felt before is gone. The farm is alive again.

The cattle are in the grass just past the edge of the barnyard.

I hear the clip-clop of the horse's hooves.

Glancing towards the sound, I see Mr. Branch leading Ms. Dolly out into their pasture. Then he heads back in, returning with Ms. Anne.

I turned toward the far side of the barnyard, squinting past the shimmer of sunlit grass. There is a building at the end of the gravel path between the barn and the house. I always heard the clucks of the chickens coming from that direction.

I can see a few fat birds walking through the grass, scratch and eating. They are bigger than the birds in the barn rafters. I could hear the soft cluck-and-coo as they fed. One sharp crow cut through them all like a barked command.

Mr. Combs was home.

I took a few steps forward, then felt Peanut bump my shoulder with his.

"Where are you going?" he asked, his hooves clacking lightly behind me.

"I need to visit Mr. Combs," I said, eyes still on the crooked fence line. "He knows things. About snakes."

Peanut's eyes went wide. "Wait—what? You're leaving the fence?" He lowered his voice to a whisper. "Mr. Branch doesn't like me doing that."

"I know," I replied. "But this matters. Mrs. Flower said he'd know what to do."

"Snakes?" Peanut blinked. "What are those?"

I let out a slow breath. "That's what I'm going to find out.

"I'm coming with you," stated Peanut.

I could see his stubborn streak rising in his eyes. It was what I was hoping to see. I liked mischief with a partner. Giving in to his wishes, I directed his actions.

"Stay close to me and don't stop until I do."

I moved towards the clear spot by the fence where I had watched Charlene this morning. There was a large gap between the dirt and the bottom wire.

"This is where we get out and come back to the barnyard," I gave instructions again. "You will go first. Then stand and wait for me to come through."

"Me, first?" Peanut's voice quivered nervously. "Then I stand and wait for you."

"On your knees, crawl through," I commanded.

I watched Peanut get down as I told him too, but I realized he couldn't crawl like a cat.

"Ok, stand up. That won't work," feeling a little frustrated.

"Stand close to the hole and let me see how far you need to bend down," I suggested.

"I think if I get on my front knees, I can crawl through partway, then squat down a little to get my backend through," Peanut suggested.

"Great. Let's do it."

Peanut got on his front knees and easily passed under the wire. Halfway through, he squatted just a bit, and he made it through.

"I made it!" exclaimed Peanut.

"We don't want to get caught," I whispered sternly at him.

I dropped to my belly and was through the hole in the blink of an eye.

Pointing with my nose, I gave directions. "We are going to run as fast as possible to the corner of that building."

"I'm ready."

"Let's go."

I started sprinting, leading Peanut to our next goal. I made it and immediately dropped to the ground in a tense crouch. Peanut dropped behind me on his front knees.

"I believe those birds are chickens and will lead us to Mr. Combs, but we don't want to sneak up on them, in case we may scare them."

"I'm ready."

We stood up. I lead, using a calm, gently stroll, towards the birds. Their heads are down, scratching at the ground. So, I give a quiet "mew" to get their attention. Bad mistake!

My mewing startled the bird, who started squawking, running in circles. Then dashed for a white box, wings flapping, loose feathers flying everywhere.

Peanut and I started following them at a short distance. I was calling, " Wait! Wait!"

Out of nowhere came this big red ball of feathers, screaming at us. "Go away! Go away!"

It jumped in the air in front of me, beating the air with its wings, while trying to claw me. Instantly, I fluffed my fur and backed away from the claws. There appeared to be a very long spike on the inside of each leg. I didn't want to be stuck by those either.

I swerved to the left and ran towards a pile of wood. I could hear Peanut pounding the earth behind me.

"Peanut, hide behind the pile. I'm going to run to the top and try to talk to this bird," I commanded.

I dashed up the wood pile stick by stick until I reached the top. I was facing the white box, looking at a tall red bird, with a little red floppy thing on top of its head and under its chin. It was marching in front of me, side to side. It looked like it fluffed its neck feathers, but it wasn't coming forward.

Gathering my wits, I tried to explain my purpose. "Hi, I'm Charlie, and my friend Peanut is hiding behind the woodpile."

"Well, you scared my hens because you were inside our boundary," said the red bird. "You're not allowed past that wood pile. Especially a cat!"

"We meant no harm. I'm looking for Mr. Combs. Mrs. Flower told me he knew about snakes," I explained in a hurry.

The red bird stopped moving, turned it's head to look at me with one eye.

After a moment, he said. "I'm Mr. Combs."

Chapter Twenty: Guardian of the Barnyard

I could hear the cackling of the hens in the white box.

"Out of nowhere, something attacked us!" cackled a hen.

"It was awful. I swear they were huge. Running right at us," claimed another.

"I couldn't tell if it was a fox or a dog chasing us," exclaimed another.

"Mr. Combs must have been asleep to let them get that close to us," claimed the first cackler.

"Yes, Yes. We need to demand better protection," came an angry voice.

"You've sure scared the hens," Mr. Combs stated, nodding his head back towards all the white box.

"Hens never run out of things to say. They cluck all day—endless streams of opinions, farm news, and gossip," Mr. Combs said, chuckling. "Now they can add being attacked by unknown creatures to their list."

"Mr. Combs, we weren't attacking the hens. We were trying to ask them how to find you," I explained.

Peanut walked around the end of the woodpile.

"Hi Mr. Combs," greeted Peanut.

Stretching his neck forward, twisting his head to look at Peanut with both eyes, Mr. Combs said, "Hmm, you don't look like a cat."

"Nope, I'm a goat. I definitely would not hurt your hens."

"Ok, you say you came to find me. What do you want?" asks Mr. Combs.

"The horses mentioned there was a snake in the pasture. Then I had a dream of a big snake eating us all up. I don't think anyone should go out to the pasture, but Mrs. Flower said there was nothing to worry about. She said you would know."

"Did I hear you say something about the pasture?" came a voice from the bottom of the woodpile.

Startled by the sudden intrusion, I sprang to my paws, while Mr. Combs fluttered his wings, looking for the voice.

"Mrs. Henrietta, what are you doing down there?" crowed Mr. Combs, all flustered.

I giggled at the sight of Mr. Combs all fluffed up to brow beat Mrs. Henrietta. His red neck feathers all fluffed up made his neck look three times bigger than normal, with his little head right in the middle staring down Mrs. Henrietta.

"Don't go getting all high and mighty with me," Mrs. Henrietta blustered right back at Mr. Combs.

Mrs. Henrietta was a pretty round red hen. Plump would be a better description. She is mad right now, and she's a flurry of red feathers.

"You're outside our boundaries," blustered Mr. Combs.

I could tell by Mr. Combs' bulging eyes he wasn't happy with Mrs. Henrietta. But Mrs. Henrietta wasn't backing down.

"Oh, hogwash! I can go anywhere I choose," snapped Mrs. Henrietta.

"What! No, you can't. How can I protect you when you're laying eggs?" blustered Mr. Combs. Clearly flustered that one hen was nesting outside his established boundaries.

"Does Mrs. Branch know you are nesting out here? No, I bet not," strained Mr. Combs, trying to make his point.

"What if a fox was on top of the woodpile instead of Charlie? Or even worse, a snake was in the woodpile waiting to eat your eggs or you?" questioned Mr. Combs.

"I trust you to be doing your job. Which means there would be no fox on top of the woodpile," Mrs. Henrietta snapped back. "But I see a cat made it to the woodpile."

"As for snakes, I better keep an eye open for them," whispered Mrs. Henrietta, bobbing her head back and forth, peering into the woodpile.

"I don't believe there are any in there right now," Mr. Combs assured her.

"That's the second time I've heard about snakes in two days," I said, bewildered by her reaction at the mention of snakes.

"They are thieves! They'll steal my eggs. Sometimes they eat them and leave the shell behind in my nest," huffed Mrs. Henrietta.

"Snakes are a menace," Mr. Combs conceded.

I frowned. So, Mrs. Flower was wrong not to be worried about them.

"I've had my share of meetings with snakes," Mr. Combs crowed. "I have a healthy respect for their wickedness," he continued. "Snakes aren't like foxes or raccoons. Foxes and raccoons can be sneaky, but you can normally see them coming," said Mr. Combs with a shake of his head.

"Snakes are slithering demons," whispered Mr. Combs, bowing his neck.

My full attention was on Mr. Combs. I crouched a little closer to the edge to get closer to Mr. Combs to hear better.

I sat with every muscle tensed, hanging on every word he said.

Mr. Comb slowly raised his head and looked me right in the eye.

It was a bone chilling stare that gave me the feeling that Mr. Combs would be a better friend than an enemy.

"Snakes are worse by far, because they slither so stealthily through the grass that you don't know they're there until it's too late," stated Mr. Combs, in a low monotone voice.

I watched as Mr. Combs' black orbs came to life and refocused on my own eyes. I felt my eyes open wide, and I cocked my ears towards Mr. Combs to absorb everything he was about to say.

"They hide in the grass, slithering up quietly to steal unsuspecting chicks or unguarded eggs," continued Mr. Combs.

I shivered. How could I protect all my new friends from these monsters?

"The one snake I fear most of all is the Rattler. Its bite is deadly. I heard one got my brother not too long ago," continued Mr. Combs.

Beside me, Peanut gasped.

"He was a hero," Mr. Combs said proudly. "He saved his coop. Rattlers have a special weapon that freezes you for a moment, just long enough for them to strike with their deadly bite," he went on.

Clearly mesmerized—and terrified—I whispered. "deadly bite."

"Yes, it has a deadly bite. You'll hear the distinctive rustle of his rattle first, if you're lucky. It uses this sound to freeze you in place," explained Mr. Combs.

"The only way to beat them is to jump like your life depends on it—because, Charlie, when you hear that rattle... it does."

I shuddered. A cold prickle crept up my spine as the weight of Mr. Combs' words settled deep in my chest.

Rattlers.

Deadly bite.

I swallowed hard Mr. Combs just confirmed my fear.

My friends could be in danger.

Then I turned to look at the cornfield, showing growth, and the hedgerow overgrown with bushes.

"Are there any rattlers in the hedgerow?" I asked, staring at the bushes lining the fence line.

Mr. Combs ruffled his feathers and shook his head. "I don't know. I've never wandered that far... but if a rattler wanted a quiet place to hide, the hedgerow would be perfect."

Chapter Twenty-One: Between Freedom and Love

"Mr. Combs, you've given me lots to think about."

"Don't get me wrong, there are some good snakes. They eat pests like insects and mice," he says, "but the bad snakes give all snakes a bad name."

I nodded, but that there are bad snakes is enough for me.

"We need to get back before we get caught outside the barnyard." I jump from the woodpile to land next to Peanut.

He beats me to the corner.

"That was pretty scary."

"Are you scanning for any sign of Mr. Branch?" I ask.

"Is the plan to run and dive under the wire where we came out?" Peanut eyed the gravel path and barnyard.

"Yes. Don't stop until we are under that wire," I command.

We're up and running. Focused on the wire in the clearing. Peanut has the lead, and I'm right on his tail.

I hear a squeaking of a hinge. I glanced at the barn door. It's closed. It must be behind us.

Peanut has kneeled to crawl under the wire. We need to get under fast, so; I ram his backside and push him through the hole as I follow him through.

We end up in a pile just on the other side of the fence in the barnyard. We made it—barely, but grinning.

I hear a voice call. "You two stinkers!"

Lying on my side, I look toward the voice to see Mrs. Branch.

She's carrying something and turns towards some poles with some wire between them.

"I didn't think to look towards the house," groaned Peanut, lying next to me.

"I didn't either," I admit as we untangle ourselves.

We both shake from head to tail, creating a mini dust cloud.

"Charlie, I'm going to go lie in the shade inside the barn," Peanut tells me.

I glance towards the pasture and see the cattle grouped out by the big tree, all lying down. But I don't see Junior.

I scan the cattle and finally notice he's off by himself on the edge of the shade from the tree.

"All seems safe," I convince myself.

I lead Peanut into the barn. I'm heading towards my favorite spot close to the milk-house wall, so I can hear the ping-ping of the barn's rhythm.

It also gives me a good view of the cattle pasture, even lying down. So, I can monitor them. In case there are snakes.

I start slowly kneading the straw into a pile for me to lie on. Peanut is using his front hooves to build his pile. Peanut kneels on his front legs, then lowers his back end to settle in for a nap.

I have no thoughts of taking a nap. I keep thinking about the information we got from Mr. Combs. I have many questions.

Is Mrs. Flower keeping a wary eye out for the slithering signs of their presence? Did she tell Junior about them? What could a snake do to Junior?

A sharp chill curled through my chest. Charlene. What could a snake do to Charlene? What if a rattler slithered unseen, lying in wait? How would a rattler with its deadly bite affect her? Would she know about jumping like a scared rabbit to get away? Fear tangled in my chest, a suffocating grip. My mind spun—snakes, Junior, Charlene. Was danger slithering closer while no one was watching?

Mr. Combs had said he'd lost his brother recently to a rattler. He'd confronted a rattler while defending his coop, losing to the deadly bite of the rattler.

That meant a rattler could be near. I knew it was unlikely he was in the pasture. If everyone else was like Mrs. Flower, and not thinking snakes were a danger, then maybe they wouldn't be careful enough.

I thought of the rooster that had died. Had the magic rattle frozen him before he could jump to get away? Would the rattle freeze me before I could get away?

It didn't matter what the snake could do to me; I had to go warn my friends.

Chapter Twenty-Two: Whispers in the Straw

I was making plans to find my way to the pasture when the barn door creaked and swung wide. Sunlight stabbed through the dust, sharp and sudden, like claws on straw.

Charlene stepped in first. Taller than before, stride all purpose. Her hair tucked beneath a worn cap, long sleeves, long pants, and the steady rhythm of her boots on the cement told me she still knew this barn. She moved with a purpose. I felt myself shrink back.

Two girls followed close behind—Indiana and Scout, Charlene's town friends. They wore bright sneakers and matching bracelets, chattering and laughing as their eyes scanned the barn with wonder. Where Charlene walked like she belonged here, these two walked like every beam and dust mote was a fresh adventure.

They froze when they saw us—me and Peanut curled in the straw like we'd always been there.

"Look at them," Indiana whispered.

"Is that a cat and a goat?" Scout asked, her head tilted. "Are they like best friends?"

"I thought Charlie was your housecat," Scout added, glancing at Charlene.

"Did you kick him out?" asked Indiana.

Charlene ignored them. "Come on, we're cutting through the barn to see Junior," snipped Charlene, still walking. "The goat's name is Peanut. He's a pygmy goat."

"But what about Charlie? I thought he was—"

Charlene spun to face her friends. "He left me—for the barn. Happy now?"

She turned back towards the horse manger door. "Let's go see Junior."

I watched Indiana and Scout look at each other, then follow Charlene towards the horses.

I curled my tail tighter against my side. I hadn't meant to hurt my friend. I just wanted to see the barn, too.

I feel Peanut stir in the straw next to me. He stands, stretches, and gives his body a little shiver to wake up.

"I thought I heard voices in my dreams," he says, still half-asleep.

"They weren't in your dreams. Charlene and her friends were here," I answer.

"Oh nice, Charlene came to see you?"

I flushed, embarrassed. "Ah, no. She was heading to see Junior."

"Do you think she'll see any snakes?" Peanut asked, as if that hadn't been on my mind already.

"Maybe. That's why I have to go out there. Nobody seems to care about the snakes, but they're dangerous."

"What! You can't go out there. What if there are snakes? And I'm not going."

"Mr. Combs said you had to jump like a rabbit to save yourself. I'm a goat."

"You're right," I said. "It's better you stay safe here." Then that would be one less friend I'd have to worry about.

Chapter Twenty-Three: The Return of Danger

A breeze stirred the weeds, then vanished. I dropped lower and stared at the boundary—the thick tangle where pasture meets wild.

Everyone I care about has crossed that line. Charlene. Her friends. Even Junior.

They moved through the resting cattle, sunlit and laughing. But I couldn't laugh. I knew what could hide in grass and shadow—sky hunters, snakes, things that don't care if you're young or kind.

They don't announce themselves. They wait.

And Junior... he wasn't moving. He stood apart. Still.

A chill slid across my spine.

I was supposed to watch the barn. But this was different. The pasture didn't belong to the barn—it belonged to whatever crept through it.

I couldn't sit and hoped someone else would notice.

I'm their protector.

The fence that once stood there had long disappeared beneath nature's creeping fingers. Twisted vines and brambles had wrapped themselves around the old, barbed wire, growing through it, over it, becoming it. What used to be a fence was now a wall of tangled branches and shadows. A hedgerow.

Its middle held no light. Just layers of old bark, bird nests, and dry spaces wide enough for something deadly to wait in silence.

It reeked of rot and feathers. Of ambush.

I couldn't go around it. I had to go through it.

I looked back toward the pasture. The town girls had wandered off with Charlene, laughing, their voices lost to distance. Junior remained—separate, small.

And very, very still.

I slipped into a trot, dust swirling around my paws as I crossed the barnyard. The breeze carried warmth from the grass and a whisper of ripe berries—summer's breath, soft and sweet.

My instincts blazed to life. My body coiled with alertness. Every rustle, every whisper of wind could be something more, and all my new friends didn't seem to notice! But none of them have experienced being attacked—twice!—like me; they didn't know what it was like to be surprised by a predator. I never wanted them to find out. If that moving grass wasn't a snake, well, then at least they'd be on alert.

My ears swiveled on high alert, picking up the smallest sounds, while my eyes stayed forward—watching for the faintest twitch of movement.

The grass was taller than I expected—thick and heavy, brushing my belly. Some stems bent beneath me; others parted around my face or tickled the length of my flanks like ghostly whiskers.

Suddenly, a flurry of feathers burst from the grass in front of me.

My heart jumped into my throat. Every hair from my ears to the tip of my tail stood straight up.

Realizing I'd startled a bird into flight, I dropped into a prone crouch and let my breathing slow. It had caught me completely off guard.

Exactly what I'd been trying to get everyone else to avoid with the snake. Some protector I am.

"Just a bird," I whispered. "You scared it more than it scared you."

I wished I'd never left the barnyard. I was safe in the barnyard.

But my friends might not be.

After a few deep breaths, I started forward again, hunting for a way through the hedgerow.

I stepped into a small clearing, where the tall grass flattened into a narrow path worn from frequent travel. It led straight to the hedgerow.

Near the bottom, there was a hole. I could see the pasture on the other side—the sunlit green beyond.

Something about it made my fur ripple. That hole felt... familiar.

I sat back on my haunches and lifted my eyes. The hedgerow rose above me like a wall of tangled branches and shadow. It breathed around the edges. Waiting.

Chapter Twenty-Four: Trust Tested

Crouching low to the ground, ears pinned flat, tail straight as a stick, I crept toward the hole.

Three steps away, I froze—flattening myself into the grass one last time to check my surroundings. Only the tip of my tail twitched, slow and steady. Every muscle wound tight, coiled like a spring. My eyes locked on the opening ahead, soaking in every shape and shadow.

It was the darkness that bothered me most.

The sunlight couldn't reach the hole's middle. It just stopped—like the light itself had second thoughts.

Was something waiting in there?

"I'll have to crouch lower. Not much room on either side. Not enough space to fight—or flee."

A chill crept down my spine.

"It could be a trap."

If I went in, I had to go straight through. No hesitation. No turning back.

"Do it fast. Get it over with," I whispered. If I wanted to protect my friends, I had no choice.

I calmed my breathing, narrowed my focus. Just me, the tunnel, and the strip of pasture light beyond.

Slowly, I lowered my hindquarters, twitching into launch position. My back legs are set. Tail aligned.

And then—go.

I exploded into motion, streaking toward the hole. My body stretched low, belly almost skimming the dirt, legs tucked into the perfect crouch.

The tunnel swallowed me.

The light vanished. The earth closed in—cool and damp, and too quiet. I surged forward—expecting anything.

A flicker. Shadow moved, or maybe I imagined it.

Instinct snapped. I flinched left—hard—clipping the side of the hedgerow.

A jolt of pain ripped across my ribs. Something sharp. A thorn? A claw?

I didn't stop to find out.

Pain and fear launched me out the other side like a rocket. I burst into the pasture, paws flying, not daring to look back.

My paws hit the pasture like thunder on dry ground. I stumbled once, but didn't stop—only when the sun found me again did I slow. Heart pounding. Ribs burning. Grass is bright and open all around me. Behind me: shadows and thorns. Ahead: Junior. And whatever came next.

I sped across the grass until I found Junior. Skidding to a halt beside him, I dropped into a crouch and scanned the open pasture. My heart thudded against my ribs like I'd been holding my breath since the hedgerow.

"Charlie, what are you doing here?" Junior asked, startled.

I gasped, finally catching enough air to speak. " I-I had to get to you."

He stepped closer, eyes wide. "Charlie... you're bleeding!"

"It's fine," I said quickly. "Just scratched myself coming through the hedgerow. Spooked myself more than anything."

Junior stared at me like I'd crossed a canyon to reach him. "You came through that thing?"

"I couldn't go around," I said. "There wasn't time. Is your mom nearby?"

He gestured toward the shade tree. "She's with the ladies—over there."

I scanned the pasture. Charlene and her friends were further out now, their laughter barely audible. Junior's eyes followed mine.

"They shouldn't be that close to the hedgerow," I muttered.

Junior tensed. "What's wrong?"

"Call your mom over," I said. "Quietly. And don't tell her I'm here."

"But—"

"Please. Just trust me."

Junior hesitated, then called out with a shaky breath. "Mom... can you come here?"

Mrs. Flower lifted her head. "What? Come over here, Junior!"

"It's important," he said, voice cracking.

After a pause, she huffed. "Alright, alright. I'm coming."

Junior stepped beside me as she began her slow approach. "She's giving me that look," he whispered. "You sure about this?"

"Absolutely," I said. "I think there is a possible danger near the hedgerow."

I looked toward the distant laughter again—and this time, the breeze didn't feel warm. It felt wrong.

Chapter Twenty-Five: A Home in Two Worlds

Mrs. Flower stormed across the pasture, her hooves striking the ground like small hammers. Her eyes locked on Junior—then shifted to me.

"What's so important that you interrupted my chewing and chat time?" Her voice was sharp enough to slice the grass.

I flinched.

So did Junior.

For a moment, doubt hit hard. What if I was wrong? What if this was just a shadow in the grass? I didn't want to lose Mrs. Flower's friendship—or look like a fool.

"Uh... hi, Mrs. Flower," I said quietly, ears down.

She stopped short, blinking as if I were an illusion. "Charlie?"

Before she could turn that glare on Junior, I stepped forward.

"This wasn't his idea," I said quickly. "He had no part in it. I just... I really needed to talk to you."

She tilted her head but stayed silent.

I swallowed hard, trying to slow the spin of my thoughts.

"I heard something. Something bad. I thought you should know."

Her ears twitched. "News? Must be serious if it brought you out of your barn and across that hedge."

"Yes, ma'am," I said, steadying my voice. "At least—I think it is."

One breath.

Then another.

"I came to warn you. There might be snakes in the pasture."

I braced myself—not just for her reaction, but for whatever came next.

A sudden scream behind me made every muscle jump.

"Snakes!" shouted Junior.

I whipped around, fur bristling. Beneath the shade tree, every cow turned its head in perfect unison—ears upright, eyes locked.

"Keep your voice down!" Mrs. Flower hissed, her glare searing straight through him.

Then her gaze flicked back to me.

"Now, Charlie," she said, snorting softly. "Snakes don't come to our pasture."

I opened my mouth, clinging to my confidence. "Mrs. Ann said she stepped on one here last summer."

Mrs. Flower scoffed. "She probably scared herself by stepping on a worm."

I blinked. That wasn't like her.

"That's not fair," I said, firmer now. "She said it frightened her."

"She would've mentioned it to me," Mrs. Flower muttered. "If it were real."

"You sent me to Mr. Combs," I said. "He believes snakes are living in the hedgerow."

Junior leaned toward me. "What's a snake?"

"Later," Mrs. Flower snapped, flicking flies from her flank. Then she looked back at me.

"What kind of snakes, Charlie?"

I hesitated. " I-I'm not sure. But Mr. Combs said something about... a rattler."

Mrs. Flower froze.

"A rattler?" she repeated. "Here?"

"That's what he said. It scared him bad."

Her stance shifted. "Did he say where?"

"No, ma'am. Just... not far."

Mrs. Flower stomped a hoof, sharp as thunder. "That's enough."

Her voice cracked like a snapping rope. "You're frightening Junior. And nearly got me worked up. Charlie, I appreciate the warning—but you can't go spreading panic. Without proof, it's just worry."

I blinked.

That stung.

More than I expected.

Chapter Twenty-Six: Bridging the Divide

A scream ripped through the air, sharp and terrified.

Mrs. Flower and I both jolted, heads snapping toward the sound.

Every hair along my spine stood on end, bristling, as if my whole body was straining to see what had caused it. Around us, every head in the pasture turned—the herd frozen mid-chew, mid-step, mid-breath.

Charlene!

She and her friends were near the pasture gate, close to the hedgerow, and she was the one who'd screamed.

She was backing away from something on the ground, her eyes locked downward, frozen in place.

Without a plan, I shot forward.

Through grass, dust, hooves—through the scattering cattle who were already breaking into a full run away from the commotion.

I ran toward it.

Toward Charlene.

Toward the thing that made her scream.

The horror on her face burned like a brand in my memory—and it pulled me forward faster than I knew I could move.

I bounded in front of her to protect her—but from what? Then I heard the rustle of dry leaves just as Charlene screeched a warning. "Look out, Charlie!"

"When you hear the rustle of the rattle, jump."

My paws exploded off the ground, and I shot towards the clouds. Something hit my hip close to my tail with such force that I spun in midair, but I landed on all four paws. Facing the snake.

Which was real.

The sound of the barnyard gate squeaking open gave me hope that Charlene had gotten away, but my full attention was on the weaving head in front of me.

The quick flicker of its forked tongue and gentle weaving of the head on the raised curve of its coiled body were mesmerizing.

Slowly, I moved around my foe, watching its yellow orbs for a sign of its intentions.

A quiver in the head was all the sign I got, but my reactions saved me.

I sprang into the air, every hair on my body reaching for the sky, lifting me higher.

The snake was incredibly fast, but missed its strike at me.

Before I could land back on my paws to leap again, the snake had struck and recoiled for another strike; it launched at me again as I landed.

My lightning-quick reflexes saved me again.

I went back into the air almost before I had touched the ground, but not quick enough. I could feel one fang graze my right front paw, spinning me in the air, to come crashing to the earth a little to the side of the snake.

This time, the snake took its time to recoil and face me.

It appeared as if the snake knew it had me right where it wanted me.

The snake flickered its tongue as if it was tasting my fear in the air, but its eyes showed no emotion.

'You are quick, little one, but not quick enough," it hissed.

My hip was becoming stiff from the initial blow, and the burning sensation in my paw was spreading.

My movement wasn't smooth and fluid anymore, more like a gimp on the front paw and a drag of the back one. I knew to stop would be deadly.

"You're mine!" hissed the snake.

He struck quicker than I could bat an eye. Its mouth was wide open, showing two huge fangs.

I didn't have time to go up into the air; I just twisted, letting the head pass close to my body, grabbing the snake's neck just behind the head in my mouth as it passed. The motion of the snake whipped me off my paws.

My surprising moved saved me from a terrible bite but infuriated the snake.

Whipping its head with such strength and force that I was whipped around, but I didn't lose my hold.

While it was flipping me in the air, the snake tried to throw its coils around me, just missing on many occasions.

Suddenly, it flipped me around, crashing me headfirst into the ground.

Stunned by the crash, I lost my hold on the snake's neck and lay helplessly on the ground.

Bursting lights and numbness were all I could see and feel.

If the snake struck now, I couldn't defend myself.

I had lost.

Chapter Twenty-Seven: Charlene's Forgiveness

A breeze brushed my fur—followed by the hiss of something slicing through the air.

Then: thump.

Whack! Whack!

The ground shook beneath me.

Before I could even lift my head, I felt arms—familiar arms—scoop me up.

Charlene.

"Watch out for the head—it can still bite you!" I heard Mr. Branch shout.

"Charlene, get Charlie to the house!"

She pulled me in close, pressing me against her chest. Her arms wrapped around me, strong and trembling. I could feel the vibrations of her steps, each one jarring my body. My paw throbbed. My hip was stiff and numb. And I was so tired.

But wrapped in her arms again—hearing her breath, feeling her heartbeat—I let go. My eyes slipped shut. Darkness wrapped around me.

I drifted in and out.

A rattle. Voices.

"Mom, open the door, please! We need to call the veterinarian—Charlie needs help!"

"I'm coming!" That was Mrs. Branch.

The door opened. I forced my eyes open and found Charlene's face looking down at me. She didn't smile.

"What happened, sweetie?" Mrs. Branch asked.

"It was a snake. A rattler." Charlene's voice broke as she carried me inside.

She laid me gently on something cool and flat—the kitchen table. Her hand stroked along my side.

"Mom, please! Call the vet now. I can't lose him."

I tried to lift my head. Nothing moved.

I could feel her hands in my fur, desperate, trembling. I couldn't purr. Couldn't blink. Couldn't reassure her.

"He's not moving," she whispered. "I'm losing him..."

More voices.

"I took care of the snake," Mr. Branch said, his voice calm.

"I called Dr. Wood," Mrs. Branch added. "She'll be here in under twenty minutes."

"Dad, I'm scared," Charlene said softly. "He's just... lying there."

"He'll be okay," Mr. Branch replied. His tone was steady. "He's banged up, but he's breathing. We'll get him help soon."

A warm hand brushed over my ears.

"Oh my god," a voice breathed. "That cat is incredible."

Somebody pulled Charlene closer, hugging us both.

"Thanks Indiana," Charlene whispered.

"I've never even seen a rattler," Indiana murmured. "I was scared you would be bitten."

I heard Scout's voice. "I didn't know what to do. I just backed away..."

"I've never been so scared," Charlene said.

"Charlene," she said, "I've never known a cat to be a protector like that. He protected you."

I was drifting.

Not fully gone, not quite awake—somewhere in a warm, heavy fog where time stretched like molasses and everything ached.

Voices came and went. Hands touched me—firm, steady, not Charlene's.

Something sharp pricked my leg. My veins went cold. Then warm. Then nothing at all.

I blinked. I think.

Shapes passed over me. Light flickered. I couldn't move my paw. Couldn't lift my head. But I could feel everything. The sting of a scratch on my front paw. A slow burn in my hip.

Cool liquid on my skin. Pressure. Something tugging—then a strange pinch. My limbs didn't obey me, but somewhere deep inside, I winced.

"She's just stitching, Charlie," I thought. "Hold still."

I could hear Charlene pacing. Her footsteps scuffed the floor like restless wings. I wanted to lift my head, flick my tail—anything to let her know I was still here.

But I couldn't.

I floated.

Then, voices sharpened. Movement. The fog thinned.

"She's smiling," someone said. No—not someone. Me. I was starting to think again.

Dr. Wood's voice filtered in, clear this time.

"Charlie was very lucky."

She said something about a fang barely nicking the muscle. No antivenom needed. Swelling was minimal. She'd left pain medicine.

I let the words roll over me, like sunshine on a worn stone.

Lucky.

She said I'd be okay.

A quiet sob escaped the air. Charlene's breath caught—then let go.

I could feel her relief like a blanket being tucked around me.

Then footsteps moved toward the kitchen.

And I knew—she was coming back.

To see me.

Chapter Twenty-Eight: Finding Home

I was awake.

Not fully—more like drifting at the edge of sleep—but enough to hear voices through the fog.

"...never in my 23 years as a veterinarian have I heard of or seen a house cat that would face one," said Dr. Wood, her voice full of wonder.

House cat?

"You still haven't," came Mr. Branch's voice, laced with amusement.

"What?" Dr. Wood asked.

"Charlie's our barn cat," he said, matter-of-fact.

I blinked—slow, deliberate. Even in this haze, I caught the faint sting in those words. Barn cat. Like a tool left hanging by the door. Functional. Replaceable.

"Well, I'll be..." Dr. Wood murmured.

Her footsteps shifted across the floor; the rustle of a coat being pulled on. Then—Charlene. Her scent moved fast through the air, warm with worry but lighter now.

"You've got yourself some barn cat, young lady. I hear he came to your defense."

I waited for the sting to come again.

But instead—

Charlene straightened.

And her voice?

It lit the air like morning sun.

"Charlie's not just any barn cat—he's the best barn cat in the world."

My ears twitched.

A different kind of ache filled my chest. Not pain.

Something else entirely.

I didn't know if I moved first or if she did—but soon Charlene's fingers brushed gently between my ears.

"You scared me, Charlie," she whispered. "But you're safe now."

I leaned into her hand, weak but willing.

Just for a moment, I let her carry the weight.

A week had passed. I was feeling like myself again.

My hip still ached, but Mr. Branch removed the stitches two days ago. I wasn't eating full meals yet—queasy lingered—but what I missed most wasn't food.

It was the barn.

Charlene had been taking care of me, just like she used to. I soaked up every moment of her attention, but deep down, I knew I couldn't stay inside forever.

I missed my walks around the barnyard. The scent of straw. The games with Junior and Peanut. The warmth of the sun across my fur. Soft cushions weren't made for creatures like me.

The barn called to me—alive, earthy, mine.

But going back meant risking something heavier than pain.

It meant hurting Charlene.

That afternoon, she came home from school and found me by the window, staring at the barn like it might vanish.

I turned to meet her gaze.

We stared at each other for the longest time, then Charlene picked me up, gave me a great big hug, and headed for the door.

Charlene entered the barn, still rubbing my ears with playful affection. She spotted her dad mid-chore and offered him a bright smile.

"Hi, Dad," she whispered.

Mr. Branch took us in, his face calm and unreadable—like always.

He nodded. "Hi, sweetie. How's everything going?"

"Just fine. School was slow, but it was okay," she said, pressing her cheek against my head, letting it linger.

Her gaze drifted to the feeding cattle. "Boy, Junior's really growing," she noted.

"Oh yes. He's doing great. He'll be a prime Black Angus bull before long," Mr. Branch replied.

Charlene reached the center of the barn aisle, glancing around. "Hey Dad... where did Charlie usually sleep?"

He smiled, keeping his eyes on his work. "Mostly in the straw with Junior, though I've seen him nap all over."

"I guess a barn cat doesn't need just one spot to call home."

"Nope," he said. "It's a big barn—with plenty of places to belong."

Charlene knelt at the far end of the parlor and gently placed me in the straw. Without realizing it, she'd chosen my favorite corner—the place I returned to most.

She stroked my chin with tender fingertips and whispered, "I'm sorry for being mad, Charlie. I love you. I was just hurt when you left the house."

She leaned closer.

"Dad told me you were special... I didn't get it before. But now I do." Her voice softened like a lullaby. "You're a barn cat, Charlie—the best barn cat in the world."

One quiet tear rolled from her cheek and landed on my nose. Not heavy. Just honest.

She sniffled and smiled—no sadness, only love. "I'll visit you every chance I get," she whispered. "I promise."

I blinked slowly, my gaze holding hers as long as I could.

With one last look, she stood, turned, and vanished through the barn door—her footsteps light, steady.

I stared after her until she disappeared, then glanced at Mr. Branch.

His weathered face held the kind of smile that didn't need words.

I curled deeper into the straw, letting warmth wrap around me, letting the barn breathe its familiar breath.

Then I heard him say—"Welcome home."

www.ingramcontent.com/pod-product-compliance
Lightning Source LLC
Chambersburg PA
CBHW042300090526
44582CB00006B/118